READ & SPEAK

CHINESE

—FOR BEGINNERS—

SECOND EDITION

The Easiest Way to Learn to Communicate Right Away!

Series Concept
Jane Wightwick

Chinese Edition
Cheng Ma

Illustrations by
Leila Gaafar

New York   Chicago   San Francisco   Lisbon   London   Madrid   Mexico City
Milan   New Delhi   San Juan   Seoul   Singapore   Sydney   Toronto

1 2 3 4 5 6 7 8 9 10 11 12 13 14 15   WDQ/WDQ   1 9 8 7 6 5 4 3 2 1 0

ISBN 978-0-07-173968-9 (book and CD package)
MHID   0-07-173968-8 (book and CD package)

ISBN 978-0-07-173967-2 (book)
MHID   0-07-173967-X (book)

Library of Congress Control Number: 2009942864

McGraw-Hill books are available at special quantity discounts to use as premiums and sales promotion, or for use in corporate training programs. To contact a representative, please e-mail us at bulksales@mcgraw-hill.com.

Enhanced CD

The accompanying disk contains audio recordings that can be played on a standard CD player. These recordings are also included in MP3 format. For iPod or similar player:

1. Insert the disk into your computer
2. Open the disk via My Computer.
3. Drag the folder "Read & Speak Chinese" into the Music Library of iTunes.
4. Sync your iPod with iTunes, then locate the files on your player under:
   ARTISTS > Chinese: Read & Speak for Beginners

Audio Flashcards

The Key Words vocabularies in this book can be studied online in interactive flashcard format at byki.com./listcentral. Search for "Read and Speak Chinese" to locate the lists.

Other titles in this series

Read and Speak Arabic for Beginners, 2nd Ed.
Read and Speak Greek for Beginners
Read and Speak Japanese for Beginners
Read and Speak Korean for Beginners

Related title:

Your First 100 Words in Chinese

CONTENTS

TOPIC 1 *What's your name?* 5
Basic greetings
Saying and asking about names

TOPIC 2 *Where are you from?* 14
Countries
Saying where you're from

TOPIC 3 *What's this?* 24
Asking about what things are
Ordering drinks and snacks

TOPIC 4 *Where is it?* 34
Describing where things are
Expressing negatives

TOPIC 5 *What's it like?* 44
Describing characteristics
Adjectives

TOPIC 6 *How do I get there?* 54
Places around town
Transportation
Directions and instructions

TOPIC 7 *Who's this?* 64
Describing your family
Possessives (*my*, *your*, etc.)
Numbers 1–10

TOPIC 8 *What do you do?* 74
Describing occupations
Talking about where you work

TEST YOURSELF 84

REFERENCE 89

ANSWERS 92

PLUS...

- 8 tear-out cards for fun games

- Audio CD for listening and speaking practice

- Online activities to enhance learning

Read & Speak **CHINESE**

Welcome to *Read & Speak Chinese*. This program will introduce you to the Chinese language in easy-to-follow steps. The Chinese you will learn is the Mandarin dialect, the most widely understood dialect of Chinese, and the "simplified" characters as used in mainland China. The focus is on enjoyment and understanding, on *reading* words rather than writing them yourself. Through activities and games you'll learn how to read and speak basic Chinese in less time than you thought possible.

You'll find these features in your program:

	Key Words	See them written and hear them on the CD to improve your pronunciation.
	Language Focus	Clear, simple explanations of language points to help you build up phrases for yourself.
	Activities	Practice what you have learned through reading, listening, and speaking activities.
	Games	With tear-out components. Challenge yourself or play with a friend. A great, fun way to review.
	Audio CD	Hear the key words and phrases and take part in interactive listening and speaking activities. You'll find the track numbers next to the activities in your book.

If you want to give yourself extra confidence with reading the script, you will find *Your First 100 Words in Chinese* the ideal pre-course companion to this program. *Your First 100 Words in Chinese* introduces the Chinese characters through 100 key everyday words, many of which also feature in *Read & Speak Chinese*.

So now you can take your first steps in Chinese with confidence, enjoyment and a real sense of progress.

Whenever you see the audio CD symbol, you'll find listening and speaking activities on your CD. The symbol shows the track number.

Track 1 is an introduction to the sounds of Chinese, including an important feature on Chinese tones. Listen to this before you start and come back to it again at later stages if you need to.

Key Words

Look at the script for each key word and try to visualize it, connecting its image to the pronunciation you hear on your CD.

2

你好 **nǐ-hǎo** — *hello*
你好 Nǐ-hǎo 你好

再见 **zài-jiàn** — *goodbye*
再见 zài-jiàn 再见

名字 **míng-zi** — *name*
名字 míng-zi

我的名字 我 的 名字
wǒ-de míng-zi — *my name*
wǒ-de míng-zi

Chinese names:

王明 **wáng míng** *(female)*
王明 wáng míng

陈天宝 **chén tiān-bǎo** *(male)*
陈天宝 chén tiān bǎo

木兰 **mù-lán** *(female)*
木兰 mù lán

黄园园 **huáng yuán-yuán** *(male)*
黄园园 huáng yuán yuán

The pronunciation next to the characters is shown in Pinyin, developed as a way of writing Chinese in Roman script. Some letters in Pinyin represent different sounds from English. We will give you tips on these sounds as they occur. In the Key Words above, **ang** is pronounced "aang" (similar to the English pronunciation of *uncle*); **z** is pronounced "ds", as in *kids*; and the **i** at the end of **míng-zi** is almost a "dummy" sound (hardly pronounced at all). The use of hyphens between syllables will help you as a beginner to break down a word into its parts.

The Chinese tones are written on the Pinyin pronunciation to help you remember them. You can read more about tones on page 91. It will take time for you to reproduce these tones. Try to mimic the native speakers on the CD as closely as you can and replay the tracks as much as possible.

Written Chinese characters offer little clue as to their pronunciation, so you should look carefully at the characters while listening to the key words, connecting the image to the pronunciation you hear on the CD. Don't expect to take it all in at once. If you find yourself using strategies such as recognizing words by how many characters they are, think of this a positive start and not as "cheating."

How do you say it?

Join the script to the Pinyin, as in the example.

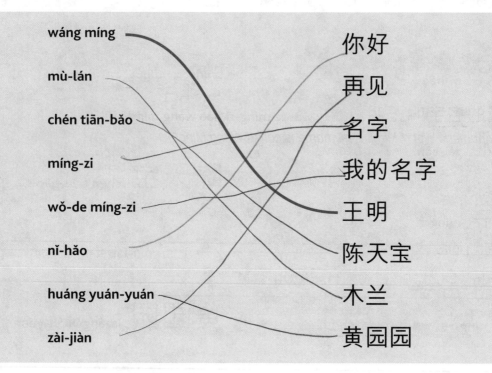

What does it mean?

Now say the Chinese out loud and write the English next to each.

你好 _hello_ 王明 _female_

再见 _goodbye_ 陈天宝 _male_

名字 _name_ 木兰 _female_

我的名字 _my name_ 黄园园 _male_

Language Focus

To form the sentence *My name is ...,* all you have to do is to add the word 叫 jiào
(*to be called*) to 我的名字 wǒ-de míng-zi (*my name*):

> 我的名字叫木兰。   **wǒ-de míng-zi jiào mù-lán.**
> *My name is Mulan. (literally, "my name is called Mulan")*
>
> 我的名字叫王明。   **wǒ-de míng-zi jiào wáng míng.**
> *My name is Wang Ming. ("my name is called Wang Ming")*

This can be shortened to:

> 我叫木兰。   **wǒ jiào mù-lán.**
> *(literally, "I called Mulan")*
>
> 我叫王明。   **wǒ jiào wáng míng.**
> *("I called Wang Ming")*

Notice that the period is written as a small circle in Chinese script: 。

You may also have noticed that there are no spaces between the characters that
form separate words or concepts. Try to identify key characters such as 我 wǒ (*I*) and
叫 jiào (*to be called*) as this will help you to split a sentence into its separate parts.

Practice introducing yourself
and learn some useful replies
on your CD.

3

What are they saying?

Write the correct number in the word balloons.

1 我的名字叫木兰。
wǒ-de míng-zi jiào mù-lán.
My Name is mulAN

2 你好, 陈天宝!
nǐ-hǎo, chén tiān-bǎo!
Hello female

3 再见。 *Goodbye*
zài-jiàn.

4 你好, 黄园园!
nǐ-hǎo, huáng yuán-yuán!
Hello name male

What do you hear?

Work out the phrases below. Then listen and check (✔)
the two phrases you hear on your audio CD.

4

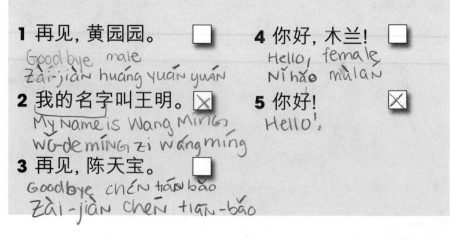

1 再见, 黄园园。 ☐
Goodbye male
Zài-jiàn huáng Yuán yuán

4 你好, 木兰! ☐
Hello, female
Nǐ hǎo mùlan

2 我的名字叫王明。 ☒
My Name is Wang Ming
wǒ-de míng zi wáng míng

5 你好! ☒
Hello!

3 再见, 陈天宝。 ☐
Goodbye chén tián bǎo
Zài-jiàn chén tian-bǎo

Key Words

5

什么? **shén-me?** *what?*

什么? what?

你叫什么名字？

nǐ jiào shén-me míng-zi? *what's your name?*

你叫什么名字？ *what name*

早上好 *good morning*

zǎo-shàng hǎo 早上好 *good morning*

ZuoshAnGhao

晚上好 *good evening*

wǎn-shàng hǎo wàn shàng hǎo

晚上好

请 **qǐng** *please*

请 qing

谢谢 **xiè-xiè** *thank you*

谢谢 xiè-xiè

In Pinyin transcription, **q** is very close to the English *ch*, as in *chimney*; **x** is close to *sh*, as in *ship*.

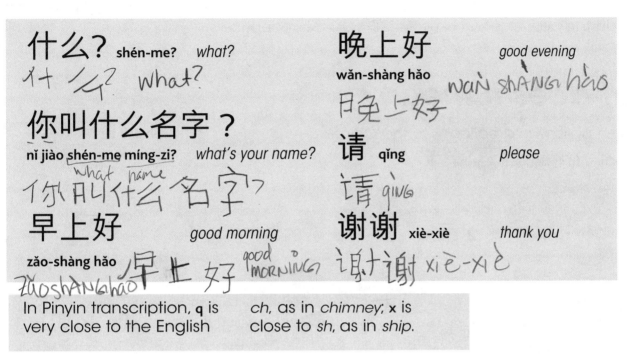

Language Focus

The Chinese word order for *What's your name?* is *"you called what name?"*:
你叫什么名字？ **nǐ jiào shén-me míng-zi**. Remember 你 **nǐ** *(you)* from 你好 **nǐ-hǎo**, which literally means *"you well"*?

nǐ -you

你叫什么名字？   **nǐ jiào shén-me míng-zi?**
What's your name?

我的名字叫木兰。   **wǒ-de míng-zi jiào mù-lán.**
My name is Mulan.

At the conference

You are registering your name at a conference.
Take part in the conversation on your CD with the receptionist.

6

What does it mean?

Match the English word balloons to the Chinese.

For example: **1d**

1 *Good morning.*

2 *Hello.*

3 *What's your name?*

4 *Please.*

5 *My name's Wang Ming.*

6 *Thank you.*

b 我的名字叫王明。

a 请。

d 早上好。

c 谢谢。

f 你好。

e 你叫什么名字？

Which word?

Write the correct number of the word in the box
to complete the conversation, as in the example.

1 晚上   4 名字叫

2 什么   5 好

3 我叫

晚上 ___5___ 。
你好，_____ 好。
我的 _____ 黄园园。你叫 _____ 名字？
_____ 陈天宝。

Language Focus

Chinese names consist of three or two characters. The first character is the surname, which is followed by the given name made up of one or two characters. The surname and the given name are written together with no gap to separate the two parts. Indeed, most Chinese people call their close friends by their full names and in the same *surname + given name* order. A Chinese person living in the West will often deliberately change the order by moving the given name to the front to suit the western culture, for example changing *Ma Cheng* to *Cheng Ma* .

English names are phonetically represented in Chinese. There are some rough rules in doing so. For example, *p* is often pronounced as **b**, and *t* sometimes as **d**, so *Peter* becomes **bǐ-dé**. Some English sounds such *th* do not exist in Chinese, so the closest approximation, **s**, is used instead.

A floating dot is used to link western first names and surnames together. Since Chinese does not allow consonant clusters (groups of consonants together), extra vowels are often needed to break the cluster. The Chinese phonetic representation of the full name for *Claire Smith*, for example, is 克莱尔·史密斯 **kè-lái-ěr shǐ-mì-sī**.

What are their names?

Look at these common English names in Chinese characters and Pinyin.
Try to memorize them by looking at the number and shape of the characters.
Then cover the English and Pinyin and see if you can remember them.

安德鲁 **ān-dé-lǔ** *Andrew*	埃米 **āi-mǐ** *Amy*
大卫 **dà-wèi** *David*	克莱尔 **kè-lái-ěr** *Claire*
约翰 **yuē-hàn** *John*	简 **jiǎn** *Jane*
彼得 **bǐ-dé** *Peter*	劳拉 **láo-lā** *Laura*
马克 **mǎ-kè** *Mark*	凯蒂 **kǎi-dì** *Katie*

In or out?

Who is in the office today and who is out at meetings? Look at the wallchart and write the names in English in the correct column, as in the example.

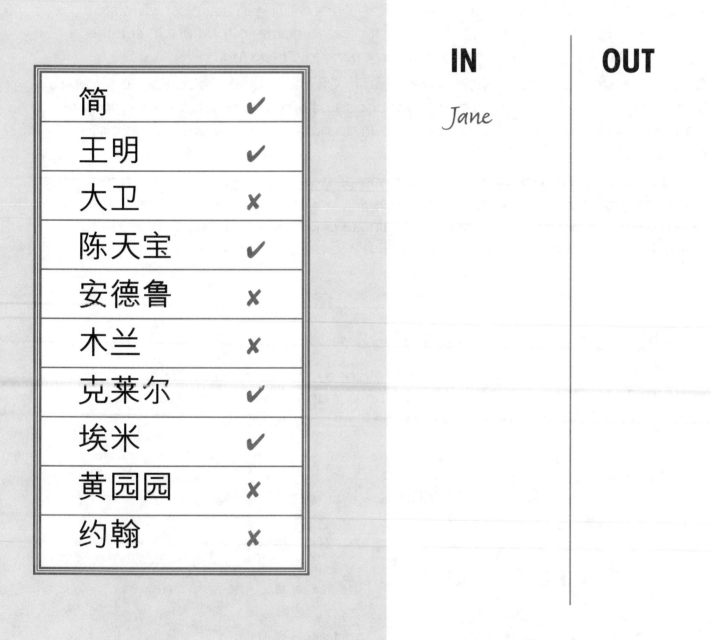

简	✔
王明	✔
大卫	✘
陈天宝	✔
安德鲁	✘
木兰	✘
克莱尔	✔
埃米	✔
黄园园	✘
约翰	✘

IN

Jane

OUT

The Name Game

1. Tear out Game Card 1 at the back of your book and cut out the name cards (leave the sentence-build cards at the bottom of the sheet for the moment).

2. Put the cards Chinese side up and see if you can recognize the names. Turn over the cards to see if you were correct.

3. Keep shuffling the cards and testing yourself until you can read all the names.

4. Then cut out the extra sentence-build cards at the bottom of the sheet and make mini-dialogs. For example:

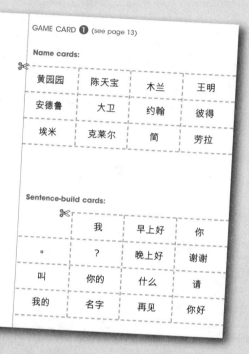

GAME CARD 1 (see page 13)

Name cards:

黄园园	陈天宝	木兰	王明
安德鲁	大卫	约翰	彼得
埃米	克莱尔	简	劳拉

Sentence-build cards:

	我	早上好	你
。	？	晚上好	谢谢
叫	你的	什么	请
我的	名字	再见	你好

| 早上好 | 。 | 你 | 叫 | 什么 | 名字 | ？ |

| 我的 | 名字 | 叫 | 木兰 | 。 |

– zǎo-shàng hǎo. nǐ jiào shén-me míng-zi?

– wǒ-de míng-zi jiào mù-lán.

黄园园
陈天宝
木兰
王明

Wang Ming
Mulan
Chen Tian-bao
Huang Yuan-yuan

5. You can also play with a friend. Make mini-dialogs for each other to read. If you both have a book, you can play Pairs (pelmanism) with both sets of sentence-build cards, saying the words as you turn over the cards.

Key Words

7

	中国 zhōng-guó	China		英国 yīng-guó	Britain
	日本 rì-běn	Japan		加拿大 jiā-ná-dà	Canada
	韩国 hán-guó	Korea		爱尔兰 ài-ěr-lán	Ireland
	美国 měi-guó	America		澳大利亚 aò-dà-lì-yà	Australia

国(家) guó (jiā)   country   城市 chéng-shì   city

国 guó means *kingdom*. The word for *China*, 中国 zhōng-guó, literally means "*middle kingdom.*" 美国 měi-guó (*America*) means "*beauty kingdom*" and 英国 yīng-guó (*Britain*) means "*heros' kingdom*"!

To learn new words, try covering the English and looking at the Chinese characters and Pinyin. Start from the first word and work your way to the last seeing if you can remember the English.

Then do the same but this time starting from the bottom and moving up to the first word. See if you can go down and up three times without making any mistakes. Then try looking only at the Chinese characters and see if you can remember the pronunciation and meaning. When you can recognize all the words, cover the Chinese and this time look at the English saying the Chinese out loud.

Where are the countries?

Write the number next to the country, as in the example.

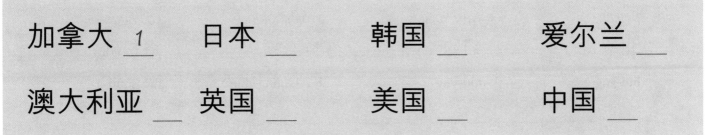

加拿大 _1_	日本 __	韩国 __	爱尔兰 __
澳大利亚 __	英国 __	美国 __	中国 __

How do you say it?

Join the English to the Pinyin and the Chinese characters, as in the example.

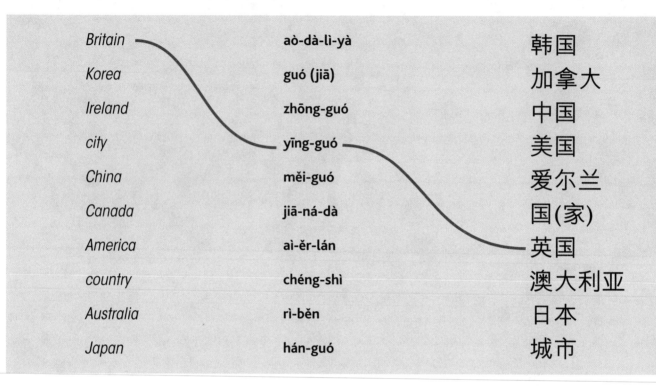

Britain	aò-dà-lì-yà	韩国
Korea	guó (jiā)	加拿大
Ireland	zhōng-guó	中国
city	yīng-guó	美国
China	měi-guó	爱尔兰
Canada	jiā-ná-dà	国(家)
America	aì-ěr-lán	英国
country	chéng-shì	澳大利亚
Australia	rì-běn	日本
Japan	hán-guó	城市

Where are the cities?

Now look at these cities and make sentences, using the word 在 **zài**, for example:
北京在中国。 **běi-jing zài zhōng-guó.** *Beijing is in China.*

Beijing	New York	Washington	Los Angeles
北京	纽约	华盛顿	洛杉矶
běi-jing	**niǔ-yuē**	**huá-shèng-dùn**	**luò-shān-jī**

Shanghai	Sydney	London	Dublin
上海	悉尼	伦敦	都柏林
shàng-hǎi	**xī-ní**	**lún-dūn**	**dū-bó-lín**

Language Focus

You can use the Chinese structure 我是 ... 人 wǒ shì ... rén ("*I'm ... person*") to mean *I'm from ...*, for example:

> 我是中国人。 wǒ shì zhōng-guó rén.
> *I'm from China./I'm Chinese.*
>
> 我是美国人。 wǒ shì měi-guó rén.
> *I'm from America./I'm American.*

To ask *Where are you from?* the question is 你是哪国人? nǐ shì nǎ guó rén? ("*you are which country's person?*"):

> 你是哪国人? nǐ shì nǎ guó rén?
> *Where are you from?*
>
> 我是加拿大人。 wǒ shì jiā-ná-dà rén.
> *I'm from Canada./I'm Canadian.*

You can also use 我是 ... 人 wǒ shì ... rén to say which town or city you're from, extending the structure to mention both country and city/town. In Chinese the sequence is always *country + city/town* and there's no need to insert any linking word between the two:

> 我是华盛顿人。 wǒ shì huá-shèng-dùn rén.
> *I'm from Washington.*
>
> 我是中国北京人。 wǒ shì zhōng-guó běi-jing rén.
> *I'm from Beijing in China.*
>
> 我是澳大利亚悉尼人。 wǒ shì aò-dà-lì-yà xī-ní rén.
> *I'm from Sydney in Australia.*

Listen to these five people introducing themselves and see if you can understand where they are from: John, Laura, Peter, Jane, Andrew.

8

Where are they from?

Join the people to the places they are from, as in the example.
Listen again to track 8 on your CD if you need to remind yourself.

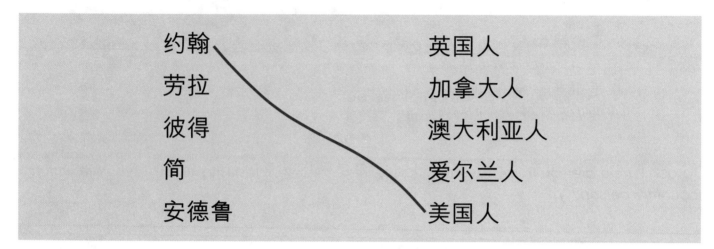

约翰	英国人
劳拉	加拿大人
彼得	澳大利亚人
简	爱尔兰人
安德鲁	美国人

Where are you from?

Now say where you're from.
Follow the prompts on your audio CD.

9

 # Key Words

10

我	wǒ	I	是	shì	to be ("am/are/is")
你	nǐ	you			
他	tā	he	人	rén	person
她	tā	she	哪?	nǎ?	which?

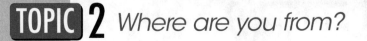
 # Language Focus

We've learned the words 我 **wǒ** *(I/me)* and 你 **nǐ** *(you)*, for example 我是 ... 人 **wǒ shì ... rén** *(I'm from ...)*; 你好 **nǐ-hǎo** *(you well)*. Now we can extend this to include 他/她 **tā** *(he/she)*, 他/她是 ... 人 **tā shì ... rén** *(He/She is from ...)*.

我是美国人。 **wǒ shì měi-guó rén.**
I'm from America./I'm American.

他是中国人。 **tā shì zhōng-guó rén.**
He's from China./He's Chinese.

她是爱尔兰人。 **tā shì aì-ěr-lán rén.**
She's from Ireland./She's Irish.

He and *she* in Chinese are written differently, but pronounced exactly the same: **tā**. 他 is *he/him*, and 她 is *she/her*.

The question forms will be:

他是哪国人？ **tā shì nǎ guó rén?**
Where is he from?

他是加拿大人。 **tā shì jiā-ná-dà rén.**
He's from Canada./He's Canadian.

她是哪国人？ **tā shì nǎ guó rén?**
Where is she from?

她是日本人。 **tā shì rì-běn rén.**
She's from Japan./He's Japanese.

Who's from where?

Make questions and answers about where these people are from.
Try to include a city that you know in the answer if you can, as in the example.

1

他是哪国人？
tā shì nǎ guó rén?
Where is he from?

他是美国纽约人。
tā shì měi-guó niǔ-yuē rén.
He's from New York in America.

2

3

4

5

6

7

8

Listen and check

Listen to the conversation on your audio CD and decide if these sentences are true or false.

		True	False
1	The conversation takes place in the morning.	☐	☐
2	The woman's name is Sophie.	☐	☐
3	She comes from Canada.	☐	☐
4	The man's name is Wang Ming.	☐	☐
5	He comes from Beijing.	☐	☐
6	They are already friends.	☐	☐

What does it mean?

Now read the Chinese you heard in the conversation and match it with English, as in the example.

I'm from Canada.	晚上好。
I'm from Shanghai.	我是加拿大人。
My name's Laura.	你好。
What's your name?	他是上海人。
Good evening.	我的名字叫劳拉。
Hello.	您叫什么名字？

What does it mean?

Try to work out each of these sentences. It will help if you break them up into the separate words and phrases. Look back at the Key Word panels if you need help.

Then read the sentences out loud when you have worked them out and write the English next to each, as in the example.

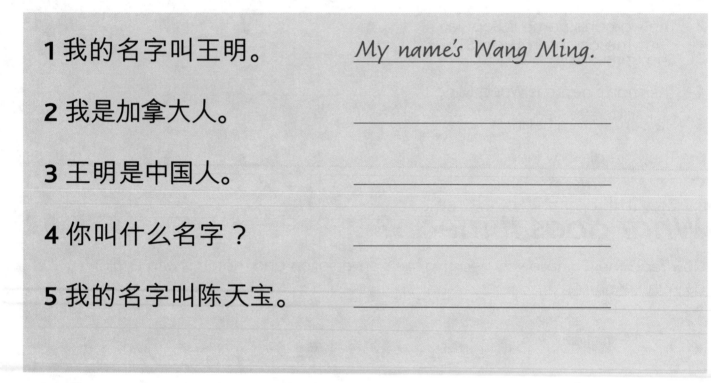

1 我的名字叫王明。   *My name's Wang Ming.*

2 我是加拿大人。   _____

3 王明是中国人。   _____

4 你叫什么名字？   _____

5 我的名字叫陈天宝。   _____

You can compare your pronunciation of the sentences with the models on your audio CD.

12

Now complete this description of yourself. Read the sentences out loud, adding your own details.

我的名字叫…

我是…

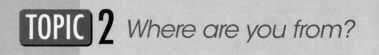

The Flag Game

1. Tear out Game Card 2.

2. Find a die and counter(s).

3. Put the counter(s) on START.

4. Throw the die and move that number of squares.

5. When you land on a flag, you must ask and answer the appropriate question for that country. For example:

   你是哪国人？ **nǐ shì nǎ guó rén?**
   Where are you from?

   我是英国人。 **wǒ shì yīng-guó rén.**
   I'm from Britain./I'm British.

6. If you can't remember the question or answer, you must go back to the square you came from. You must throw the exact number to finish.

7. You can challenge yourself or play with a friend.

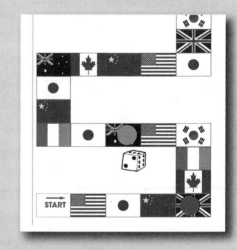

Key Words

椅子	yǐ-zi	chair		门	mén	door
桌子	zhuō-zi	table		窗子	chuāng-zi	window
电视	diàn-shì	television		笔	bǐ	pen
书	shū	book		杂志	zá-zhì	magazine
包	bāo	bag		沙发	shā-fā	sofa
电脑	diàn-nǎo	computer		电话	diàn-huà	telephone

13

Listen first to the key words on your CD. Then look around the room you're in and try to use the words to name as many objects as you can find. Count how many Chinese words you use.

When reading Chinese, it often helps to identify characters which reoccur in a number of words. For example the character 电 diàn meaning *electric* occurs in three of the key words on this page:

电话 diàn-huà (*telephone*, literally "electric speaking")

电视 diàn-shì (*television*, literally "electric watching")

电脑 diàn-nǎo (*computer*, literally "electric brain")

What does it mean?

Match the Chinese with the pictures, then write the Pinyin and the English, as in the example.

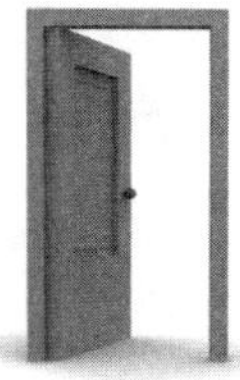

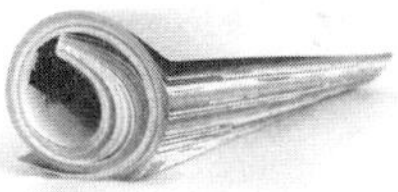

电话 _____

书 包 _____

电脑 _____

窗 子 _chuāng-zi (window)_

门 _____

电视 _____

笔 _____

椅 子 _____

桌 子 _____

杂志 _____

沙发 _____

Word Square

Can you find the 8 key words in the word square?
Circle them and write the English, as in the example.

直	侄	植	电	话	忍	惹	子
蜘	脂	嘿	耗	鹤	直	合	何
阂	貉	盒	黑	浩	电	妊	蓉
认	电	脑	熔	壬	沙	发	融
纫	视	忍	电	种	峙	炙	子
子	置	椅	中	杂	志	蛊	质
疵	桌	子	丛	匆	电	终	忠
电	雌	凑	词	窗	子	赐	聪

telephone _____

_____

_____

_____

_____

_____

_____

Odd One Out

Which is the odd one out? Circle the word that doesn't belong in each row.

中国 * 电话 * 美国 * 英国

杂志 * 书 * 晚 * 电视

木兰 * 王明 * 彼得 * 笔

你好 * 名字 * 再见 * 早上好

桌子 * 窗子 * 沙发 * 名字

Language Focus

To ask *What's this?* the structure in Chinese is *"this is what?."*

> 这是什么？ **zhè shì shén-me?** *What's this?*

To answer this question use 这是... **zhè shì....** Notice that Chinese does not have a direct equivalent of *a/an*, neither does it have plurals.

> 这是椅子。 **zhè shì yǐ-zi.** *This is (a) chair.*
>
> 这是电话。 **zhè shì diàn-huà.** *This is (a) telephone.*

To form a question, just add the word **ma** (吗) at the end of the statement:
这是 ...吗？ **zhè shì ...ma?** *(Is this ...?).*

> 这是椅子吗？ **zhè shì yǐ-zi ma?** *Is this is (a) chair?*
>
> 这是电话吗？ **zhè shì diàn-huà ma?** *Is this is (a) telephone?*

There are no simple equivalents of *yes* and *no* in Chinese. They vary according to the context. The best way to say *yes* is just to repeat the main verb in the previous question. The best way to say *no* is to use the word 不 **bú** (meaning *not*) followed, again, by the main verb in the question. So, to answer the questions above, you could say:

> 是。 **shì.** *(Yes) it is.*
>
> 不是。 **bú shì.** *(No) it isn't.*

Ask and answer the questions.
Follow the prompts on your CD.

14

What's this?

Look at the photos of everyday objects from unusual angles. Then read the sentences and decide which picture they describe, as in the example.

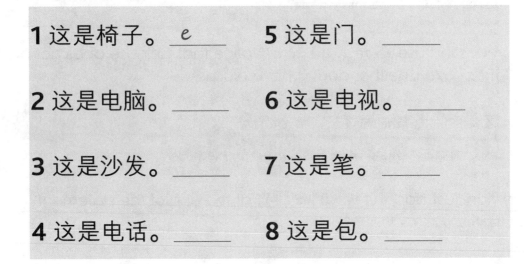

1 这是椅子。 _e_

2 这是电脑。 _____

3 这是沙发。 _____

4 这是电话。 _____

5 这是门。 _____

6 这是电视。 _____

7 这是笔。 _____

8 这是包。 _____

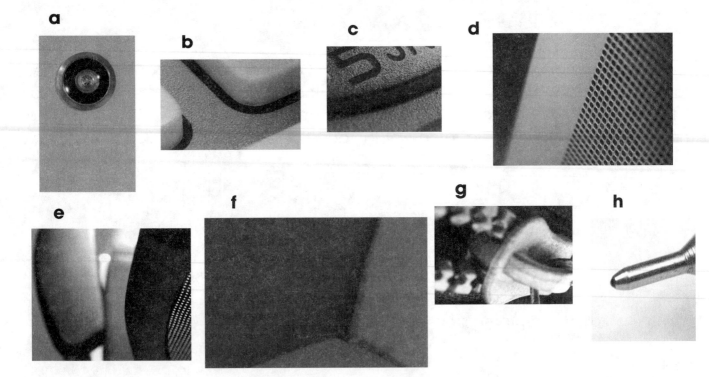

a

b

c

d

e

f

g

h

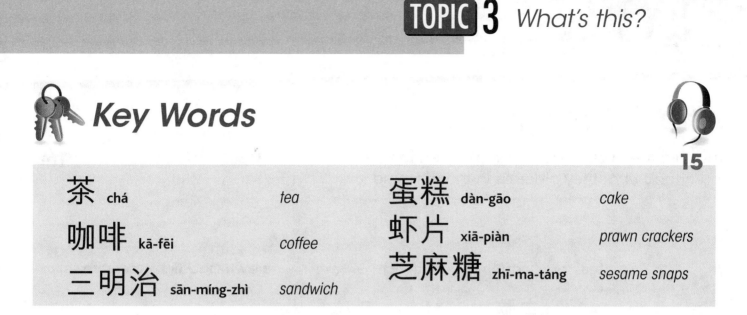

Key Words

15

茶	chá	tea		蛋糕	dàn-gāo	cake
咖啡	kā-fēi	coffee		虾片	xiā-piàn	prawn crackers
三明治	sān-míng-zhì	sandwich		芝麻糖	zhī-ma-táng	sesame snaps

Language Focus

To say *I'd like...*, you can use 我想要点... **wǒ xiǎng yào diǎn...**, for example. If you want two things, simply link them with 和 **hé** (pronounced as in the English *her* but without the 'r' sound):

我想要点茶。 **wǒ xiǎng yào diǎn chá.** *I'd like a tea.*

我想要点虾片。 **wǒ xiǎng yào diǎn xiā-piàn.** *I'd like some prawn crackers.*

我想要点咖啡和三明治。 **wǒ xiǎng yào diǎn kā-fēi hé sān-míng-zhì.**
I'd like some coffee and a sandwich.

An alternative is to use the phrase: 请给我... **qǐng gěi wǒ...** *(Please give me...)*. Note that the word 请 **qǐng** *(please)* cannot be used at the end of a sentence. Adding 好吗？ **hǎo ma?** *(may I ask?)* at the end will make the request more polite:

请给我咖啡(好吗?) **qǐng gěi wǒ kā-fēi (hǎo ma?)** *Please give me coffee (may I ask?)*

请给我芝麻糖(好吗?) **qǐng gěi wǒ zhī-ma-táng (hǎo ma?)**
Please give me some sesame snaps (may I ask?)

The equivalent of *here you are* (when handing over something) is ...来了 **...lái le** *(... comes)*:

咖啡来了。 **kā-fēi lái le.** *"Here comes the coffee."*

椅子来了。 **yǐ-zi lái le.** *"Here comes the chair."*

Who orders what?

What are the customers ordering? Listen to your CD
and check what they order, as in the example.

16

	tea	coffee	sandwich	cake	prawn crackers	sesame snaps
Customer 1	✓				✓	
Customer 2						
Customer 3						
Customer 4						
Customer 5						

Now look at the table and pretend you are ordering for yourself. Try to use the
two ways you know of asking for something:

我想要点茶和虾片。 wǒ xiǎng yào diǎn chá hé xiā-piàn.

请给我茶和虾片，好吗？ qǐng gěi wǒ chá hé xiā-piàn, hǎo ma?

Unscramble the conversation

Can you put this conversation in the correct order?

你好。我想要点咖啡。 **a**
nǐ-hǎo. wǒ xiǎng yào diǎn kā-fēi.

谢谢。 **b**
xièxiè

芝麻糖来了,咖啡和芝麻糖。 **c**
zhī-ma-táng lái le, kāfēi hé zhī-ma-táng.

是的。这是什么？ **d**
shì-de. zhè shì shén-me?

这是芝麻糖。 **e**
zhè shì zhī-ma-táng.

咖啡？ **f**
kā-fēi?

请给我一块芝麻糖。 **g**
qǐng gěi wǒ yī-kuài zhī-ma-táng.

早上好。 **h**
zǎo-shàng hǎo.

ORDER: _h,_ _____

Now check your answer with the conversation on your audio CD.

17

At the café

Your turn to order now. Look at the menu below and then you'll be ready to order from the waitress on your CD.

茶

咖啡

三明治

蛋糕

虾片

芝麻糖

The Café Game

1. Cut out the picture cards from Game Card 3.

2. Put the cards into a bag.

3. Shake the bag.

4. Pull out a card without looking.

5. Ask for the item on the card. For example:

   我想要点茶。
   wǒ xiǎng yào diǎn chá.
   I'd like a tea.

6. If you can ask the question out loud quickly and fluently, then put the card aside. If not, then put it back into the bag.

7. See how long it takes you to get all of the cards out of the bag. Or play with a friend and see who can collect the most cards.

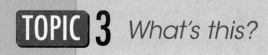

Key Words

房间	**fáng-jiān**	room	房子	**fáng-zǐ**	house
电冰箱	**diàn-bīng-xiāng**	refrigerator	树	**shù**	trees
橱柜	**chú-guì**	cupboard	车	**chē**	car
炉子	**lú-zǐ**	stove	猫	**māo**	cat
床	**chuáng**	bed	狗	**gǒu**	dog
照片	**zhào-piàn**	picture	小鼠	**xiǎo-shǔ**	mouse

19

Chinese words can be a single character, such as 车 **chē** (car) or 树 **shù** (trees). But more often they are a combination of two or more characters.

For example, 小鼠 **xiǎo-shǔ** (mouse) consists of two characters: 小 **xiǎo** meaning small and 鼠 **shǔ** meaning rodent. Looking out for common characters can help you remember vocabulary.

What does it mean?

Join the Chinese to the Pinyin and write down what the words mean in English.

照片   diàn-bīng-xiāng _____
狗   gǒu   _____
房子   xiǎo-shǔ   _____
猫   chuáng   _____
床   zhào-piàn   ___*picture*___
电冰箱   fáng-zǐ   _____
车   shù   _____
树   māo   _____
房间   chē   _____
小鼠   chú-guì   _____
橱柜   lú-zǐ   _____
炉子   fáng-jiān   _____

What can you see?

Look at the picture and check (✔) the
things you can see, as in the example.

猫 ☑   车 ☐
包 ☐   窗子 ☐
树 ☐   炉子 ☐
床 ☐   橱柜 ☐
电话 ☐   照片 ☐
电冰箱 ☐   电视 ☐
书 ☐   电脑 ☐
车 ☐   笔 ☐
桌子 ☐   杂志 ☐

 **Key Words**

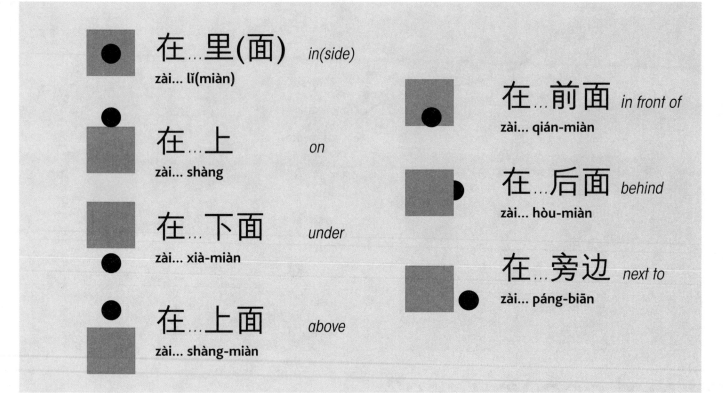

在…里(面) *in(side)*
zài… lǐ(miàn)

在…上 *on*
zài… shàng

在…下面 *under*
zài… xià-miàn

在…上面 *above*
zài… shàng-miàn

在…前面 *in front of*
zài… qián-miàn

在…后面 *behind*
zài… hòu-miàn

在…旁边 *next to*
zài… páng-biān

 **Language Focus**

When describing the position of something, you use the word 在 **zài** before the place as well as the appropriate positional word after. For example:

在桌子上 **zài zhuō-zi shàng** *on the table* ➔
笔在桌子上。 **bǐ zài zhuō-zi shàng.** *The pen is the table.*

在床后面 **zài chuáng hòu-miàn** *behind the bed* ➔
小鼠在床后面。 **xiǎo-shǔ zài chuáng hòu-miàn.** *The mouse is behind the bed.*

Practice saying where things are on your CD.

21

Which word?

Put a circle around the word that correctly
describes each picture, as in the example.

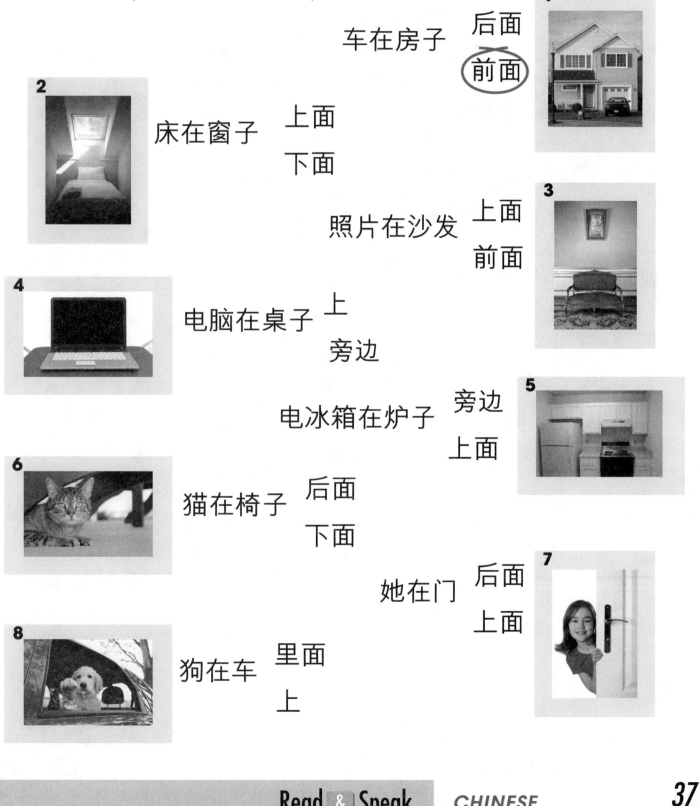

车在房子 后面
⟨前面⟩

床在窗子 上面
下面

照片在沙发 上面
前面

电脑在桌子 上
旁边

电冰箱在炉子 旁边
上面

猫在椅子 后面
下面

她在门 后面
上面

狗在车 里面
上

 **Language Focus**

The Chinese equivalent of the English *there's a/there are some...* is 有 **yǒu**, meaning *to have*. The word order is:

place + positional word + 有 **yǒu** *(have) + object*

The Chinese word order is virtually like saying the English backwards!

> 桌子上有笔。 zhuō-zi shàng yǒu bǐ.
>
> *There's a pen on the table. (table + on + have + pen)*
>
> 床下面有小鼠。 chuáng xià-miàn yǒu xiǎo-shǔ.
>
> *There's a mouse under the bed. (bed + under + have + mouse)*

To form the question *is there a/are there some...?* simply add 吗? **ma?** on the end:

> 橱柜里面有包吗？ chú-guì lǐ-miàn yǒu bāo ma?
>
> *Is there a bag in the cupboard? (cupboard + in + have + bag + **ma?**)*
>
> 椅子下面有小鼠吗？ yǐ-zi xià-miàn yǒu xiǎo-shǔ ma?
>
> *Is there a mouse under the chair? (chair + under + have + mouse + **ma?**)*

> Look around the room you are in at the moment, or think of a room you know well. Can you describe where some of the things are using 有 **yǒu**?

Where are the mice?

See how many mice you can find in the picture and make sentences about them using the sentence table, as in the example.

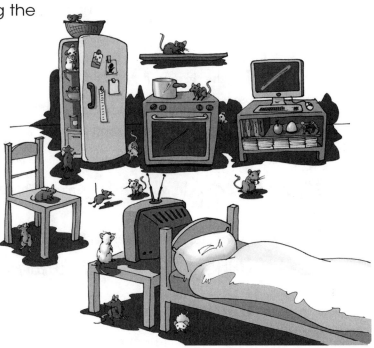

Example:

床下面有小鼠。

chuáng xià-miàn yǒu xiǎo-shǔ.

There's a mouse under the bed.

桌子 zhuō-zi

椅子 yǐ-zi

电冰箱 diàn-bīng-xiāng

沙发 shā-fā

橱柜 chú-guì

炉子 lú-zǐ

电视 diàn-shì

电脑 diàn-nǎo

床 chuáng

里 lǐ

上面 shàng-miàn

下面 xià-miàn

后面 hòu-miàn

上 shàng

旁边 páng-biān

前面 qián-miàn

有小鼠

yǒu xiǎo-shǔ

Language Focus

The simplest way to express the negative in Chinese is to add 不 **bú**. You can make the following sentences negative in this way:

> 这是狗。 **zhè shì gǒu.** *It's a dog.*
>
> 这不是狗。 **zhè bú-shì gǒu.** *It's not a dog.*
>
> 我是日本人。 **wǒ shì rì-běn rén.** *I'm from Japan.*
>
> 我不是日本人。 **wǒ bú-shì rì-běn rén.** *I'm not from Japan.*
>
> 照片在床上面。 **zhào-piàn zài chuáng shàng-miàn.** *The picture is above the bed.*
>
> 照片不在床上面。 **zhào-piàn bú zài chuáng shàng-miàn.** *The picture isn't above the bed.*

Note that the opposite of 有 **yǒu** is 没有 **méi-yǒu**:

> 沙发后面有小鼠。 **shā-fā hòu-miàn yǒu xiǎo-shǔ.**
> *There's a mouse behind the sofa.*
>
> 沙发后面没有小鼠。 **shā-fā hòu-miàn méi-yǒu xiǎo-shǔ.**
> *There isn't a mouse behind the sofa.*

No it isn't!

Practice disagreeing! Go to your audio CD and contradict all the statements you hear.

22

True or False?

Decide if the sentences describing the picture are true or false.

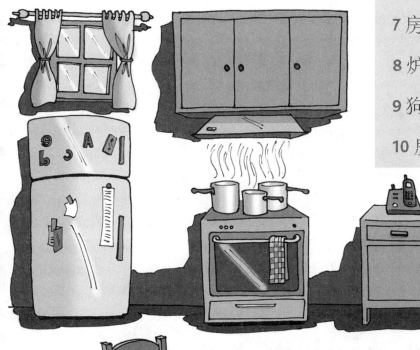

	True	False
1 房间里有电冰箱。	☑	☐
2 房间里有床。	☐	☐
3 电话在桌子上。	☐	☐
4 有两个橱柜。	☐	☐
5 有两个窗子。	☐	☐
6 桌子下面没有小鼠。	☐	☐
7 房子后面有树。	☐	☐
8 炉子在电冰箱旁边。	☐	☐
9 狗在桌子下面。	☐	☐
10 房间里没有电视。	☐	☐

Language Review

You're half way through this program – congratulations! This is a good time to summarize the main language points covered so far in *Read & Speak Chinese*.

1 There are no plural differences in Chinese; 门 **mén** can mean either *door* or *doors*.

2 是 **shì** means *to be (am/is/are)*. You can use this with different nouns or pronouns, e.g. 我 **wǒ** *(I)*, 你 **nǐ** *(you)*, 他/她 **tā** *(he/she)*.

> 我是美国人。 **wǒ shì měi-guó rén.** *I'm from America./I'm American.*
>
> 这是电话。 **zhè shì diàn-huà.** *This is (a) telephone.*

3 You can ask for something by using the phrase 我想要点… **wǒ xiǎng yào diǎn…** *(I'd like…)* or 请给我… **qǐng gěi wǒ…** *(Please give me…)*.

4 To describe position, the word 在 **zài** is used before the place. Prepositions *(in/on/under, etc.)* in Chinese are placed *after* nouns rather than in front as in English. *There is/there are* is expressed by 有 **yǒu** *(to have)* in Chinese. Notice these simple Chinese structures in comparison with the English:

The book is on the table./	书	在	桌子	上 。
Books are on the table.	books	zài	table	on
There is a bed in the room./	房间	里	有	床 。
There are beds in the room.	room	in	have	bed

5 *Yes/No* questions are formed by adding 吗? **ma?** at the end of sentences. Other simple questions can be formed using 什么? **shén-me?** *(what)* or 哪? **nǎ?** *(which?)*. Two negatives are used: 没 **méi** (before the verb 有 **yǒu** – *to have*) and 不 **bú** (before other verbs).

> 这是什么？ **zhè shì shén-me?** *What's this?*
>
> 这不是狗吗？ **zhè bú shì gǒu ma?** *Isn't it a dog?*
>
> 房间里没有床。 **fáng-jiān lǐ méi-yǒu chuáng.** *There isn't a bed in the room.*

My Room

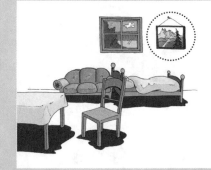

1. Tear out Game Card 4 at the back of your book and cut out the the small pictures of items around the house (leave the sentence-build cards at the bottom of the sheet for the moment).

2. Stick the pictures wherever you like on the scene below.

3. Cut out the sentence-build cards from Game Card 4. Make as many sentences as you can describing your room. For example:

床	上面	有	照片	。

chuáng shàng-miàn yǒu zhào-piàn.

Sentence-build cards:

里	上	下面	上[
电视	旁边	后面	前[
。	橱柜	有	没有
房间	窗子	桌子	椅子
三明治	照片	电话	床
猫	狗	小鼠	电脑

Key Words

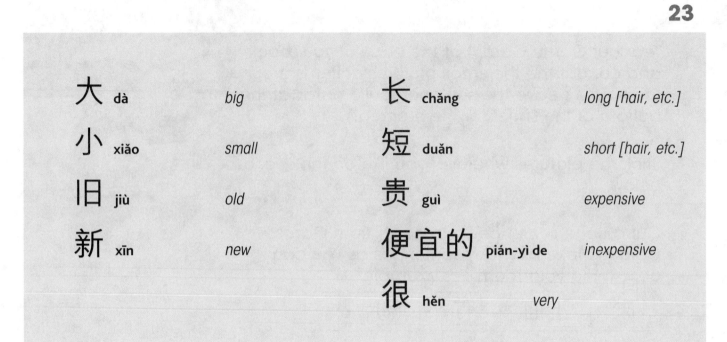

大	dà	big	长	chǎng	long [hair, etc.]
小	xiǎo	small	短	duǎn	short [hair, etc.]
旧	jiù	old	贵	guì	expensive
新	xīn	new	便宜的	pián-yì de	inexpensive
			很	hěn	very

Language Focus

Adjectives (descriptive words) come before the noun described as in English:

旧椅子 jiù yǐ-zi *(an) old chair*

小杯 xiǎo bēi *(a) small cup*

The position of 很 hěn *(very)* is the same as in English, coming before the adjective. Notice the addition of 的 de in the first phrase, linking the adjective to what it is describing.

很旧的椅子 hěn jiù de yǐ-zi *a very old chair*

房子很小。 fáng-zi hěn xiǎo. *The house (is) very small.*

Can you remember?

Cover the Key Words panel on page 44. Then see if you can write out the Pinyin and meaning of the words below, as in the example.

便宜的   p *ián-yi* d *e*   *inexpensive*

长   c _ _ _ g   _____

小   _ _ _ o   _____

旧   j _ _   _____

很   _ _ n   _____

短   _ u _ _   _____

贵   g _ _   _____

大   _ _   _____

新   _ ī _   _____

What does it mean?

Match the Chinese with the pictures. Then read the Chinese out loud and write the English next to each, as in the example.

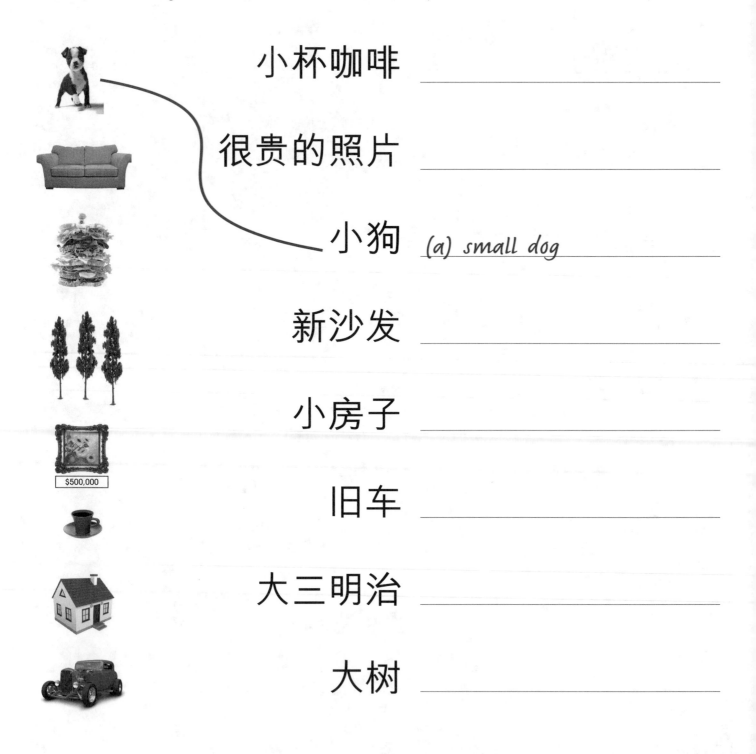

小杯咖啡 _____

很贵的照片 _____

小狗 *(a) small dog* _____

新沙发 _____

小房子 _____

旧车 _____

大三明治 _____

大树 _____

Listen and check

Listen to the conversation at the car rental company and decide if these sentences are true or false.

24

		True	False
1	The conversation takes place in the evening.	☐	☐
2	The woman wants to rent a car.	☐	☐
3	She thinks the first car is very expensive.	☐	☐
4	She thinks the second car is too big.	☐	☐
5	She likes the third car.	☐	☐

Unscramble the sentences

Look at the scrambled sentences below and write the correct order.

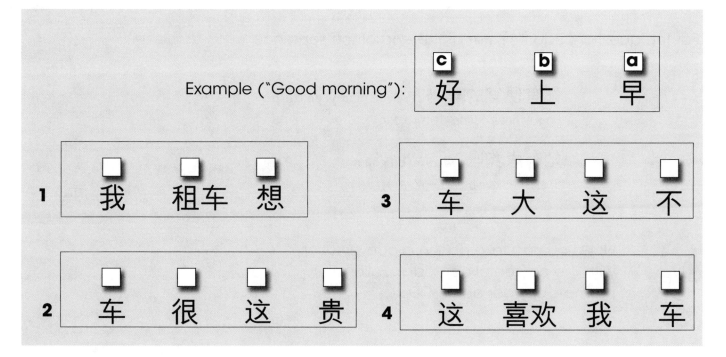

Example ("Good morning"):

c	b	a
好	上	早

1

☐	☐	☐
我	租车	想

2

☐	☐	☐	☐
车	很	这	贵

3

☐	☐	☐	☐
车	大	这	不

4

☐	☐	☐	☐
这	喜欢	我	车

Language Focus

You already know that Chinese uses the word 有 **yǒu** *(to have)* for *there is/there are*. 有 **yǒu** can also be used with personal pronouns to express possession:

> 我有 **wǒ yǒu** *I have*
>
> 你有 **nǐ yǒu** *you have*
>
> 他/她有 **tā yǒu** *he/she has*

You can combine these possessive phrases with the new language you have learned in this topic:

> 我有大车。 **wǒ yǒu dà chē.** *I have a big car.*
>
> 你有小房子。 **nǐ yǒu xiǎo fáng-zi.** *You have a small house.*
>
> 木兰有新电脑。 **mù-lán yǒu xīn diàn-nǎo.** *Mulan has a new computer.*

For the question, add 吗? **ma?** at the end of the sentence.

> 你有便宜的车吗? **nǐ yǒu pián-yì de chē ma?**
> *Do you have an inexpensive car?*
>
> 她有大狗吗? **tā yǒu dà gǒu ma?**
> *Does she have a big dog?*

Now you can take part in a conversation with the car rental company. Follow the prompts on your audio CD.

25

Key Words

26

腿 tuǐ	leg		头发 tóu-fǎ	hair
胳膊 gē-bo	arm		头 tóu	head
手指 shǒu-zhǐ	fingers		鼻子 bí-zi	nose
眼睛 yǎn-jīng	eyes		嘴 zuǐ	mouth
耳朵 ěr-duo	ears		肚子 dù-zi	stomach

By now you're probably feeling much more confident about reading and speaking Chinese. Maybe you'd like to try writing the characters for yourself. Although it's fun to copy the simpler ones, you will need to get a guide to writing simplified Chinese characters in order to form them correctly. The strokes should be completed in a certain order and you will need plenty of practice to get it right.

Which word?

Circle the correct word to match the translation, as in the example.

1	*head*	耳朵	(头)	小房	头发
2	*leg*	嘴	长	腿	胳膊
3	*stomach*	手指	短	狗	肚子
4	*mouth*	椅子	眼睛	车	嘴
5	*fingers*	手指	很	耳朵	的
6	*hair*	胳膊	大	头	头发
7	*ears*	耳朵	鼻子	旧	肚子
8	*nose*	眼睛	树	鼻子	车
9	*eyes*	胳膊	短	狗嘴	眼睛
10	*arm*	贵	胳膊	吗	头

At the pet show

Can you use the words in the box to complete the description of these pets?

1 短	**2** 有	**3** 耳朵
4 小	**5** 狗	**6** 头发

这猫 2 很长的＿＿＿，长腿和＿＿＿鼻子。

这＿＿＿有＿＿＿头发，很长的＿＿＿和大眼睛。

What does he look like?

What does the creature look like? Make as many sentences
as you can describing what it looks like.

We've included some extra vocabulary you could use in your description.

Example:

他很胖。他有长尾巴。

tā hěn pàng. tā yǒu cháng wěi-ba.

He's fat. He has a long tail.

尾巴 **wěi-ba** *tail*

翅膀 **chì-bǎng** *wings*

很胖 **hěn pàng** *to be fat*

很瘦 **hěn shòu** *to be thin*

美丽的 **měilì-de** *beautiful*

丑陋的 **chǒu-lòu-de** *ugly*

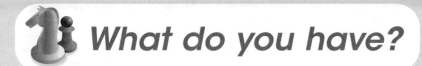

What do you have?

(1) Cut out the picture cards from Game Card 5 and put them in a bag.

(2) Cut out set 2 adjective cards and put them in a different bag.

(3) Pull out one card from each bag without looking.

(4) Make a sentence to match the cards you have chosen, for example:

我有旧电脑。

wǒ yǒu jiù diàn-nǎo.
(I have an old computer.)

(5) Keep playing until all the cards have been chosen.

(6) You can put the cards back in the bag and start again – each time the sentences will be different.

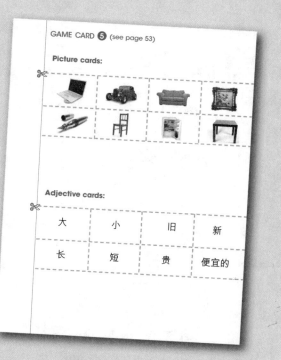

GAME CARD **5** (see page 53)

Picture cards:

Adjective cards:

| 大 | 小 | 旧 | 新 |
| 长 | 短 | 贵 | 便宜的 |

旧

Key Words

机场 **jī-chǎng**	airport	停车场 **tíng-chē-chǎng**	parking lot
学校 **xué-xiào**	school	桥 **qiáo**	bridge
酒店 **jiǔ-diàn**	hotel	街 **jiē**	street
银行 **yín-háng**	bank	长安街 **cháng-ān jiē**	Changan Street
餐馆 **cān-guǎn**	restaurant		
车站 **chē-zhàn**	station	在那里 **zài nà-lǐ**	over there

28

You are new in town and are asking a Chinese-speaking friend about the facilities. Follow the prompts on your audio CD.

Questions and answers

Match the questions with their answers, as in the example.

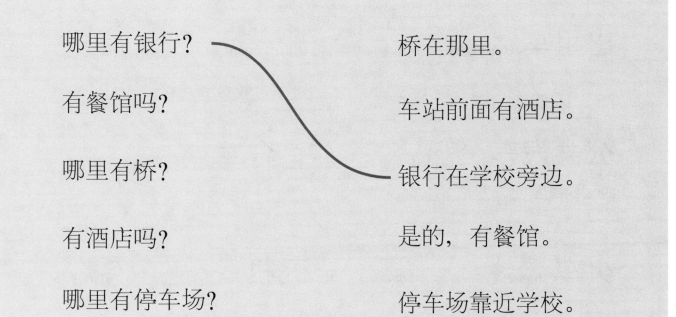

哪里有银行?   桥在那里。

有餐馆吗?   车站前面有酒店。

哪里有桥?   银行在学校旁边。

有酒店吗?   是的,有餐馆。

哪里有停车场?   停车场靠近学校。

Key Words

29

出租车 **chū-zū chē**   *taxi*   船 **chuán**   *boat*

公共汽车   *bus*   自行车 **zì-xíng-chē**   *bicycle*

gōng-gòng qì-chē

火车 **huǒ-chē**   *train*   飞机 **fēi-jī**   *plane*

Language Focus

To express how you travel, use 坐 **zuò** (*travel by*) ┐ means of transportation:

坐车 **zuò chē** *by car*

坐火车 **zuò huǒ-chē** *by train*

坐公共汽车 **zuò gōng-gòng qì-chē** *by bus*

坐船 **zuò chuán** *by boat*

Word Square

Can you find the 7 different means of transportation in the word square?
Write out the Pinyin and meaning for the words you have found, as in the example.

直	侄	植	电	话	忍	飞	机
车	脂	嘿	耗	鹤	好	合	何
阂	貉	火	车	浩	电	妊	蓉
认	电	脑	熔	壬	沙	出	融
纫	船	忍	赐	种	崎	租	子
子	自	行	车	杂	志	车	质
疵	桌	子	丛	匆	电	终	忠
电	雌	公	共	汽	车	赐	电

fēi-jī (plane)

_____

_____

_____

_____

_____

_____

Language Focus

The two characters 车 **chē** (*vehicle*) and 机 **jī** (*machine*) are basic building blocks for many other concepts:

公共汽车 **gōng-gòng qì-chē** *"public vehicle", i.e. bus*

出租车 **chū-zū chē** *"vehicle for hire", i.e. taxi*

火车 **huǒ-chē** *"fire vehicle", i.e. train*

飞机 **fēi-jī** *"flying machine", i.e. plane*

 *Key Words*

请问 **qǐng-wèn**	*excuse me!*	坐火车 **zuò huǒ-chē**	*(go) by train*
去...怎么走？ **qù ... zěn-me zǒu?**	*How do I get to ...?*	坐出租车 **zuò chū-zū-chē**	*(go) by taxi*
转 **zhuǎn**	*turn*	然后 **rán-hòu**	*then*
右 **yòu**	*right*	接着 **jiē-zhe**	*after that*
左 **zuǒ**	*left*	博物馆 **bó-wù-guǎn**	*museum*
照直走 **zhào-zhí zǒu**	*go straight ahead*	公共汽车站 **gōng-gòng qì-chē zhàn**	*bus stop*

Ask for directions to places around town. Follow the prompts on your audio CD.

31

Language Focus

The Chinese sounds **you** and **zuo** show how tones play an important part in distinguishing different meanings.

We have learned from the previous units that 有 **yǒu** means *to have* or *there is*. In this meaning **yǒu** should be pronounced in the 3rd tone (falling–rising). However, 右 **yòu** pronounced in the 4th tone (falling), means *right* as in 转右 **zhuǎn yòu** *(turn right)*.

Similarly, 左 **zuǒ** in the 3rd tone means *left* as in 转左 **zhuǎn zuǒ** *(turn left)*. But it when pronounced 坐 **zuò** in the 4th tone it means *(go) by*, as in 坐出租车 **zuò chū-zū-chē** *(by taxi)*. Listen again to these key phrases opposite and try to reproduce the tones:

坐火车 **zuò huǒ-chē** *(go) by train*

坐出租车 **zuò chū-zū-chē** *(go) by taxi*

转左 **zhuǎn zuǒ** *turn left*

转右 **zhuǎn yòu** *turn right*

The question 去...怎么走？ **qù ... zěn-me zǒu?**, used to ask *How do I get to...?*, literally means *"go...how from here"*:

去长安街怎么走？**qù cháng-ān jiē zěn-me zǒu?**
How do I get to Changan Street?

去机场怎么走？**qù jī-chǎng zěn-me zǒu?**
How do I get to the airport?

Which way?

Make questions and answers, as in the example.

去车站怎么走？ **qù chē-zhàn zěn-me zǒu?**
How do I get to the station?

转左。 **zhuǎn zuǒ.**
Turn left.

1

2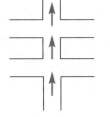

3

4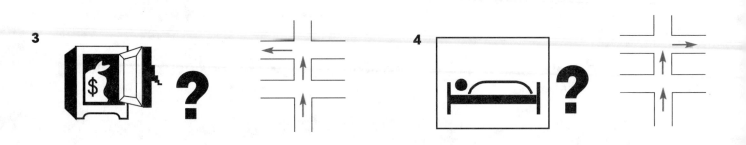

5

6

Around town

Below is a plan of a small town with some landmarks shown.

Starting from **You are here** try to give directions to the following places:

医院	酒店	公园	公共汽车站
yī-yuàn	**jiǔ-diàn**	**gōng-yuán**	**gōng-gòng qì-chē zhàn**
the hospital	*the hotel*	*the park*	*the bus stop*

For example, your directions to the station could be something like this:

照直走。接着转右。医院在桥旁边。

zhào-zhí zǒu. jiē-zhe zhuǎn yòu. yī-yuàn zài qiáo páng-biān

Go straight ahead. After that turn right. The hospital is next to the bridge.

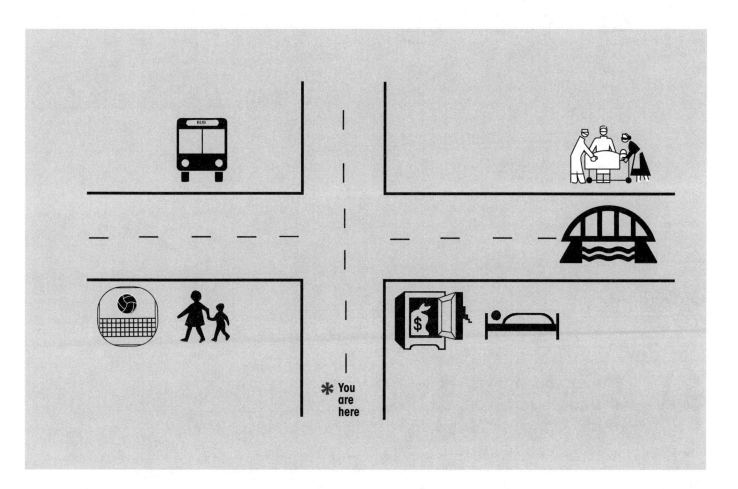

Unscramble the conversation

Can you put this conversation in the correct order?

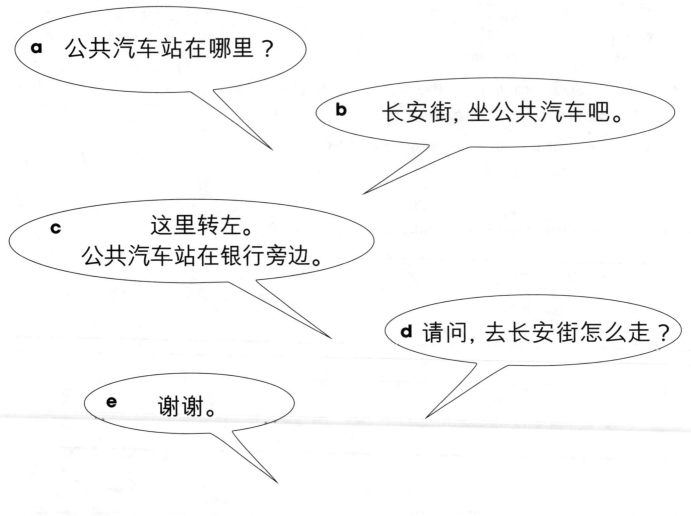

a 公共汽车站在哪里？

b 长安街，坐公共汽车吧。

c 这里转左。
公共汽车站在银行旁边。

d 请问，去长安街怎么走？

e 谢谢。

ORDER: *d,* _____

Check your answer with the conversation on your audio CD.

32

Town Planning

1. Cut out the pictures of places around town from Game Card 6.

2. Listen to the first set of directions for the bank on your audio CD.

3. Pause the CD and stick the picture of the bank in the correct place on the town map on your game card.

4. Listen to the next set of directions and stick down the appropriate picture.

5. Repeat for all the directions until you have all your pictures stuck down on the map.

6. Looking at the completed map, you could try to give directions to the various places yourself. For example:

照直走。接着转左。银行在右边，
在学校旁边。

zhào-zhí zǒu. jiē-zhe zhuǎn zuǒ. yín-háng zài yòubiān, zài xué-xiào páng-biān

Go straight ahead. After that turn left. The bank is on the right, next to the school.

Key Words

太太 **tài-tai**	*wife*	
先生 **xiān-shēng**	*husband*	
妈妈 **mā-ma**	*mother (mom)*	
爸爸 **bà-ba**	*father (dad)*	
姐姐 **jiě-jie**	*older sister*	

妹妹 **mèi-mei**	*younger sister*	
哥哥 **gē-ge**	*older brother*	
弟弟 **dì-di**	*younger brother*	
孩子 **hái-zi**	*children*	
女儿 **nǚ-ér**	*daughter*	
儿子 **ér-zi**	*son*	

Find some family photographs and point to your relatives and friends, saying who they are in Chinese.

For example:

我的妈妈 **wǒ-de mā-ma** *my mom*

我的姐姐 **wǒ-de jiě-jie** *my older sister*

 # Language Focus

You can talk about your family using the language you already know:

我有哥哥。 **wǒ yǒu gē-ge.**
I have an older brother.

我有女儿。 **wǒ yǒu nǚ-ér.**
I have a daughter.

我没有妹妹。 **wǒ méi yǒu mèi-mei.**
I don't have a younger sister.

我没有孩子。 **wǒ méi yǒu hái-zi.**
I don't have any children.

What does it mean?

Join the English to the Pinyin and the Chinese characters, as in the example.

English	Pinyin	Chinese
children	**mèi-mei**	女儿
husband	**mā-ma**	妹妹
older brother	**xiān-shēng**	孩子
daughter	**jiě-jie**	哥哥
father (dad)	**hái-zi**	姐姐
mother (mom)	**tài-tai**	儿子
older sister	**nǚ-ér**	弟弟
younger brother	**gē-ge**	爸爸
wife	**bà-ba**	先生
younger sister	**ér-zi**	太太
son	**dì-di**	妈妈

 Language Focus

Remember that to form possessives in Chinese, all you have to do is to add the character 的 **de** after the personal pronoun or name:

> 我的妈妈 **wǒ-de mā-ma** *my mom*
>
> 你的姐姐 **nǐ-de jiě-jie** *your older sister*
>
> 她的弟弟 **tā-de dì-di** *her younger brother*
>
> 他的爸爸 **tā-de bà-ba** *his dad*
>
> 王明的房子 **wáng-míng-de fáng-zi** *Wang Ming's house*
>
> 她是木兰的妈妈。 **tā shì mùlán-de mā-ma.** *She is Mulan's mom.*

In colloquial Chinese 的 **de** is often omitted:

> 我妈妈 **wǒ mā-ma** *my mom*
>
> 你姐姐 **nǐ jiě-jie** *your older sister*

To make a pronoun plural, i.e., to change *my* to *our* or *he* to *they,* the character 我 **men** is added after the singular:

> 我 **wǒ** *I*   →   我们 **wǒ-men** *we*
>
> 我的 **wǒ-de** *my*   →   我们的 **wǒ-men-de** *our*
>
> 你 **nǐ** *you (singular)*   →   你们 **nǐ-men** *you (plural)*
>
> 你的 **nǐ-de** *your (singular)*   →   你们的 **nǐ-men-de** *your (plural)*
>
> 他/她 **tā** *he/she*   →   他/她们 **tā-men** *they*
>
> 他/她的 **tā-de** *his/her*   →   他/她们的 **tā-men-de** *their*
>
> 这是我们的电脑。 **zhè shì wǒ-men-de diàn-nǎo.** *This is our computer.*
>
> 这是你们的房子吗？ **zhè shì nǐ-men-de fángzi ma?** *Is this your (plural) house?*
>
> 这是他们的电视。 **zhè shì tā-men-de diàn-shì.** *This is their television.*

Family Tree

Make sentences about this family, as in the example.

木兰是王明的太太。

mù-lán shì wáng-míng-de tài-tai.

Mulan is Wang Ming's wife.

王明

木兰

陈天宝

黄园园

David's family

Listen to David answering questions about his family. Circle the correct names, as in the example. (Look at page 11 if you need to review English names.)

35

约翰
安德鲁
马克

克莱尔
简
劳拉

大卫
约翰
彼得

马克
安德鲁
彼得

Questions and answers

Now read the questions on the right and then match them to the answers on the left that David gave, as in the example.

你叫什么名字？	他的名字叫安德鲁。
你妈妈叫什么名字？	她的名字叫克莱尔。
我爸爸叫什么名字？	我的名字叫大卫。
你是哪里人？	有，我有哥哥。
你有姐姐吗？	他的名字叫彼得。
你有哥哥吗？	我是美国纽约人。
哥哥叫什么名字？	我没有姐姐。

Language Focus

To introduce someone, you can say:

她叫简。 **tā jiào jiǎn.**
This is Jane. ("she called Jane")

这是我的姐姐，她叫简。 **zhè shì wǒ-de jiě-jie, tā jiào jiǎn.**
This is my older sister, (she's called) Jane.

To ask **Who's this?**, the Chinese structure is *"he/she is who"*: 他/她是谁？ **tā shì shuí?**

When introduced, you can respond with the expression you heard earlier in this course: 高兴见到你，王明 **gāo-xìng jiàn dào nǐ.**

So now we can put all that together into a short conversation:

你好，王明。 **ní-hǎo, wáng-míng.**
Hello, Wang Ming.

你好，简。他是谁？ **nǐ-hǎo, jiǎn. tā shì shuí?**
Hello Jane. Who's this?

这是我的弟弟马克。 **zhè shì wǒ-de dì-di, mǎ-kè.**
This is my younger brother, Mark.

你好，马克。高兴见到你。 **nǐ hǎo, mǎkè. gāo-xìng jiàn dào nǐ.**
Hello Mark. Pleased to meet you.

高兴见到你，王明。 **gāo-xìng jiàn dào nǐ, wáng-míng.**
Pleased to meet you, Wang Ming.

Now introduce <u>your</u> family. Follow the prompts on your audio CD.

36

TOPIC 7

 **Key Words**

一	**yī**	*one*	六	**liù**	*six*
二/两	**èr/liǎng**	*two*	七	**qī**	*seven*
三	**sān**	*three*	八	**bā**	*eight*
四	**sì**	*four*	九	**jiǔ**	*nine*
五	**wǔ**	*five*	十	**shí**	*ten*

 **Language Focus**

Chinese characters for numbers 1 to 10 are relatively simple in terms of the number of strokes. You can also use the western numerals (1, 2, 3, etc.) in Chinese, but the pronunciations still need to be memorized. The best strategy is to learn the characters first and associate the pronunciations with the characters.

Notice the two variants of *two*. 二 **èr** is the mathematical number. However, when it comes to counting a specific number of people or things, 两 **liǎng** must be used.

When counting something specific, you also need to add a "measure word." This word is put after the number and varies depending on what is being counted. For the moment you can stick to 个 **gè**, which is a general purpose measure word:

> 我有三个孩子。 **wǒ yǒu sān-gè háizi.** *I have three children.*
>
> 我有两个姐姐。 **wǒ yǒu liǎng-gè jiě-jie.** *I have two older sisters.*
>
> 我有一个弟弟。 **wǒ yǒu yī-gè dìdì.** *I have one younger brother.*

How many?

Match the numbers with the figures, as in the example.

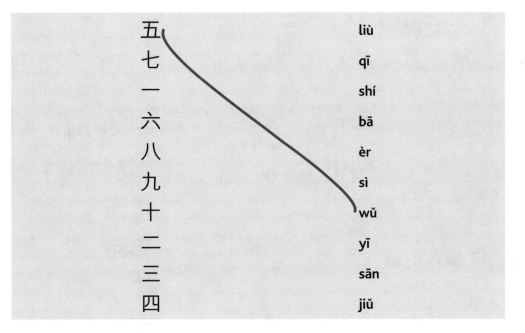

Chinese sums

Circle the correct answer to these sums, as in the example.

		一	二	三	四	五	六	七	八	九	十
1	一 + 二 =	一	二	③	四	五	六	七	八	九	十
2	四 + 二 =	一	二	三	四	五	六	七	八	九	十
3	二 x 三 =	一	二	三	四	五	六	七	八	九	十
4	五 + 三 =	一	二	三	四	五	六	七	八	九	十
5	六 – 二 =	一	二	三	四	五	六	七	八	九	十
6	七 + 三 =	一	二	三	四	五	六	七	八	九	十
7	九 – 四 =	一	二	三	四	五	六	七	八	九	十
8	八 + 一 =	一	二	三	四	五	六	七	八	九	十
9	三 x 三 =	一	二	三	四	五	六	七	八	九	十
10	六 – 五 =	一	二	三	四	五	六	七	八	九	十

My family

Use the table below to make sentences about yourself, as in the examples

我有两个姐姐。 **wǒ yǒu liǎng-gè jiě-jie.** *I have two older sisters.*

我没有孩子。 **wǒ méi yǒu hái-zi.** *I don't have any children.*

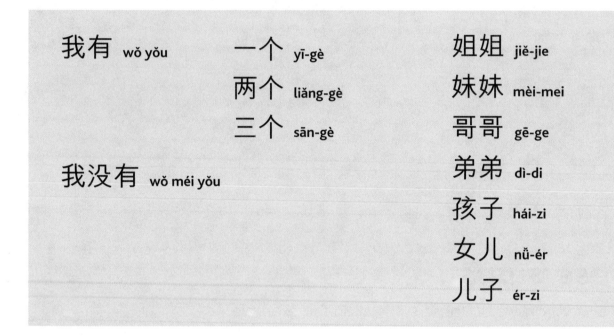

我有 wǒ yǒu	一个 yī-gè	姐姐 jiě-jie
	两个 liǎng-gè	妹妹 mèi-mei
	三个 sān-gè	哥哥 gē-ge
我没有 wǒ méi yǒu		弟弟 dì-di
		孩子 hái-zi
		女儿 nǚ-ér
		儿子 ér-zi

Listen and speak

Now imagine you are with some of your family looking for the station and you meet a Chinese friend.

38

Prepare carefully the information below you will need to take part in the conversation. Then go to your audio CD and see how you get on introducing your family.

1 Think of two members of your family – one male and one female. For example, your husband and your daughter; or your brother and your mother.

2 How would you tell someone their names in Chinese?

3 How would you ask *How do I get to the station?*

4 How do you say *thank you* and *goodbye*?

You can repeat the conversation, but this time use two different members of your family and ask how to get to the bus stop.

 **Bingo!**

1. Cut out the small number tokens and the bingo cards on Game Card 7.

2. Find 16 buttons for each player or make 16 small blank pieces of card (to cover the squares on the bingo card).

3. Put the tokens into a bag and shake thoroughly.

4. Pull out a number token and say the number out loud in Chinese.

5. If you have that number on your card, cover the square with a button or blank piece of card. If you have more than one square with that number, you can only cover one.

6. Put the number token back in the bag and shake again.

7. Repeat steps 3–6 until you have all the squares covered on the bingo card. Then you can shout:
   我赢啦！ wǒ yíng lā! (*I've won!*)

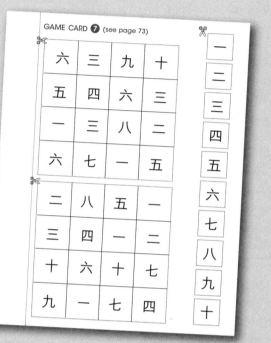

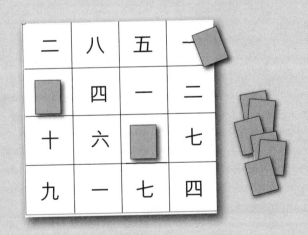

 **Key Words**

39

老师	lǎo-shī	*teacher*	司机	sī-jī	*driver*
学生	xué-shēng	*student*	厨师	chú-shī	*chef*
医生	yī-shēng	*doctor*	演员	yǎn-yuán	*actor*
文职人员 wén-zhí rén-yuán		*office worker*	工程师 gōng-chéng-shī		*engineer*
商店助手 shāng-diàn zhù-shǒu		*store assistant*	会计师 kuài-jì-shī		*accountant*

If your occupation or those of your family aren't listed here, try to find out what they are in Chinese.

What does it mean?

Join the Chinese to the Pinyin and the English, as in the example.

Chinese	Pinyin	English
工程师	yǎn-yuán	office worker
医生	xué-shēng	accountant
演员	yī-shēng	actor
厨师	lǎo-shī	driver
文职人员	chú-shī	store assistant
老师	wén-zhí rén-yuán	engineer
商店助手	gōng-chéng-shī	doctor
司机	kuài-jì-shī	cook/chef
学生	sī-jī	teacher
会计师	shāng-diàn zhù-shǒu	student

The tools of the trade

Match the jobs to the tools of the trade, as in the example.

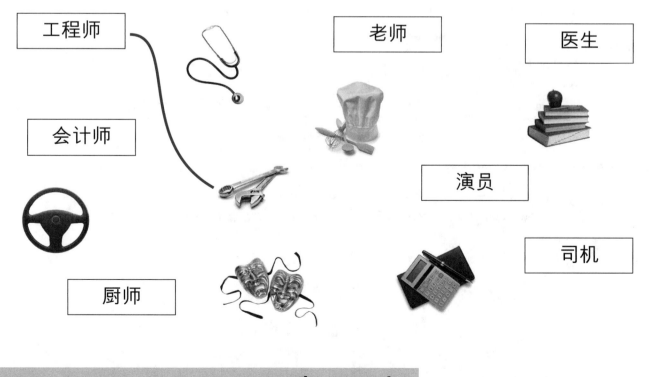

 ## *Language Focus*

To ask someone about their job in Chinese, you can use the question:

你做什么工作？ **nǐ zuò shén-me gōng-zuò?** *("you do what job?")*.

To answer this, just say 我是 **wǒ shì** *(I am)* + *occupation*. There's no need for *a/an*, and occupations don't change for male/female:

你做什么工作？ **nǐ zuò shén-me gōng-zuò?**
What do you do?

我是演员。 **wǒ shì yǎn-yuán.**
I'm an actor.

我是学生。 **wǒ shì xué-shēng.**
I'm a student.

Other possible answers include:

我在家工作。 **wǒ zài jiā gōng-zuò.**
I work from home.

我退休了。 **wǒ tuì-xiū le.**
I'm retired.

我目前不工作。 **wǒ mù-qián bú gōng-zuò.**
*I'm not working at the moment. (*目前 **mù-qián** = *at the moment/currently)*

40

Listen and note

Listen to two people telling you about themselves and fill in the details in English on the forms below.

Name: ....*Wang Ming*................

Nationality: ....

Name of spouse: ....

No. of children: ....

Occupation: ....

Name: ....

Nationality: ....

Name of spouse: ....

No. of children: ....

Occupation: ....

Your turn to speak

Now you give same information about yourself.
Follow the prompts on your audio CD.

Read & Speak   *CHINESE*

What's the answer?

Match the questions to the answers.

For example: **1d**

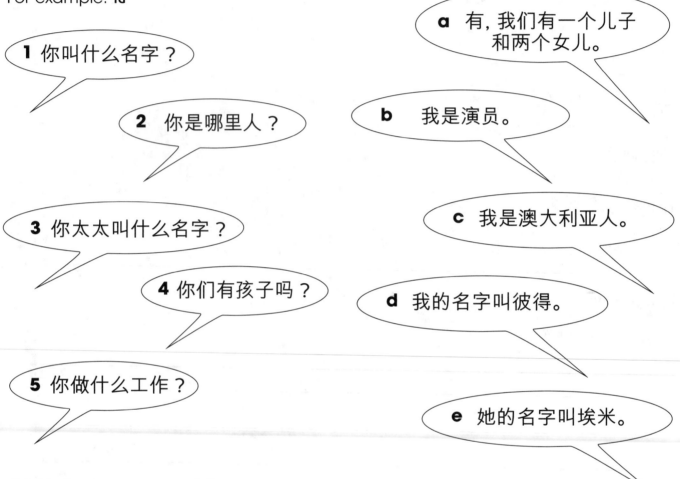

1 你叫什么名字？

2 你是哪里人？

3 你太太叫什么名字？

4 你们有孩子吗？

5 你做什么工作？

a 有，我们有一个儿子和两个女儿。

b 我是演员。

c 我是澳大利亚人。

d 我的名字叫彼得。

e 她的名字叫埃米。

Which word?

Write the correct number of the word in the box
to complete the description, as in the example.

1 孩子 **2** 两个 **3** 名字

4 有 **5** 演员 **6** 埃米

我的 _3_ 叫彼得, 我是____。
我是澳大利亚人。你太太的
名字叫____。我们____三个
____：一个儿子和____女儿。

 # Key Words

42

工厂	**gōng-chǎng**	*factory*	办公室	**bàn-gōng-shì**	*office*
医院	**yī-yuàn**	*hospital*	学院	**xué-yuàn**	*college/ university*
商店	**shāng-diàn**	*store*			
剧院	**jù-yuàn**	*theater*			

Look back as well at the Key Words on page 54 for other places of work.

 ## Language Focus

To say *I work in...* you can use 我在...工作 **wǒ zài ... gōng-zuò**:

> 我是医生。我在北京的医院工作。
> **wǒ shì yī-shēng. wǒ zài běi-jīng de yī-yuàn gōng-zuò.**
> *I am a doctor. I work in a hospital in Beijing.*

Note that 的 **de** is again used to link the nouns, in this case, *hospital* and *Beijing*. Without **de** the meaning is different: 北京医院 **běi-jīng yī-yuàn** means *Beijing Hospital*.

To find out where someone works, you can ask:

> 你在哪里工作？
> **nǐ zài nǎ-lǐ gōng-zuò?**
> *Where do you work?*

TOPIC 8

Word Square

Can you find the 8 different work places in the word square?
Words can read horizontally or vertically.
Write out the meaning for the words you have found.

疵	佺	植	工	厂	忍	惹	子
蜘	脂	学	耗	鹤	好	合	何
阆	貉	院	黑	浩	电	妊	蓉
银	行	院	熔	壬	沙	发	店
纫	视	忍	电	种	崎	炙	子
厂	剧	椅	商	店	志	学	校
医	院	子	丛	匆	电	终	忠
电	雌	厂	词	窗	办	公	室

factory _____

_____

_____

_____

_____

_____

Now make sentences for each of the work places, as in the example:

我是工程师。我在工厂工作。

wǒ shì gōng-chéng-shī. wǒ zài gōng-chǎng gōng-zuò.

I am an engineer. I work in a factory.

80

What are they saying?

Match the people with what they are saying. For example: **1d**

1 我在纽约的学校工作。

2 我在北京的餐馆工作。

3 我在美国的银行工作。

4 我在伦敦的商店工作。

5 我在加拿大的剧院工作。

6 我在爱尔兰的工厂工作。

a b c

d e f

Listen and speak

Imagine you are a chef. You're meeting someone for the first time and they are asking you about yourself.

43

Prepare carefully the information below you will need to take part in the conversation. Then go to your audio CD and see how you get on talking about yourself.

1 Your name is Wang Ming (王明).

2 You're from Beijing.

3 You're a chef.

4 You work in a Chinese restaurant in New York.

5 You have two daughters.

6 Your wife is a teacher in a big school.

Which word?

Now write the correct number of the word in the box to complete the description, as in the example. (Note: 但是 **dàn-shì** = *but*)

1 太太	**2** 学校	**3** 厨师
4 老师	**5** 工作	**6** 女儿

我的名字叫王明。我是 *3* 。我是北京人，但是我在纽约的餐馆____。我____木兰是____。她在____工作。

我们有两个____，他们是学生。

Where do I work?

GAME CARD **8** (see page 83)

Picture cards:

Profession cards:

会计师	司机	医生	厨师
商店助手	学生	演员	文职人员
老师	工程师		

(1) Tear out the work-place picture cards and profession word cards on Game Card 8.

(2) Turn the cards face down on a table, with the pictures on one end of the table and the words on the other.

(3) Turn over a word card and say ... 我是... wǒ shì ... (*I'm a/an ...*) as appropriate, e.g.:

我是老师。 wǒ shì lǎo-shī. (*I'm a teacher*).

(4) Then turn over a picture card. If the work-place picture matches the profession, say

我在学校工作。 wǒ zài xué-xiào gōng-zuò.
(*I work in a school*).

(5) If you turn over a matching picture and say both sentences correctly you get to keep the cards. If you don't, you must turn the cards face down and try again.

(6) The winner is the one who collects the most cards.

(7) You can compete with a friend or challenge yourself against the clock.

(Review the vocabulary on pages 54, 56 and 74 before you play the game.)

TEST YOURSELF

This *Test Yourself* section reviews all the Chinese you have learned in this program. Have a go at the activities. If you find you have forgotten something, go back to the relevant topic(s) and look again at the *Key Words* and *Language Focus* panels.

May I have...?

Ask for the following, as in the example:

请给我茶, 好吗? **qǐng gěi wǒ chá, hǎo ma?**

1

2

3

4

5

6

7

Listen and check

Listen to Huang Yuan-yuan talking about herself and decide if the following sentences are true or false.

		True	False
1	Huang Yuan-yuan is Chinese.	☐	☐
2	She comes from a small town.	☐	☐
3	She's a teacher.	☐	☐
4	She works in France.	☐	☐
5	Her husband is an engineer.	☐	☐
6	She has five children.	☐	☐

Which word?

Now write the correct number of the word in the box to complete the description of Huang Yuan-yuan, as in the example.

1 医生	**2** 老师	**3** 儿子	**4** 女儿
5 四	**6** 英国	**7** 大	**8** 中国

我叫黄圆圆，我是上海人，上海是__8__的一个大城市。

我是____，我在____的中文学校工作。我先生是____，

他在中文学校旁边的一家____医院工作。我们有____

个孩子，一个____和三个____。

Can you try and make up a similar description about yourself?

Read and check

Look at the picture and decide if the sentences are true or false.
Look back at topics 4–6 if you are unsure of any of the words.

	False	True
图片里有医院。	☐	☐
医院的右边有学校。	☐	☐
医院的左边没有银行。	☐	☐
街上有狗。	☐	☐
街上没有车。	☐	☐
车上有小猫。	☐	☐
学校后面有大树。	☐	☐
银行前面有一辆旧自行车。	☐	☐

What does it mean?

Can you remember these words? Join the words and write the Pinyin
next to the Chinese, as in the example.

children	儿子	*ér-zi*
husband	先生	
son	女儿	
daughter	爸爸	
father	妈妈	
mother	姐姐	
younger sister	妹妹	
older brother	哥哥	
older sister	弟弟	
wife	太太	
younger brother	孩子	

How do you say it?

Now see if you can say these in Chinese, as in the example.

1 My husband is a doctor.
我先生是医生。
wǒ xiān-shēng shì yī-shēng.

2 I have four children.

3 His son is an engineer.

4 Mulan's mother is from Shanghai.

5 My wife's name is Claire.

6 Her younger brother is an actor.

7 I don't have any older sisters.

8 I have three daughters.

44

At the tourist office

Finally, you are going to test your new Chinese conversational skills by joining in the dialog on your audio CD.

You're going to ask for some information at a tourist information office.

To prepare, first see if you can remember these words and phrases. Write the Pinyin and the English next to the Chinese, as in the example.

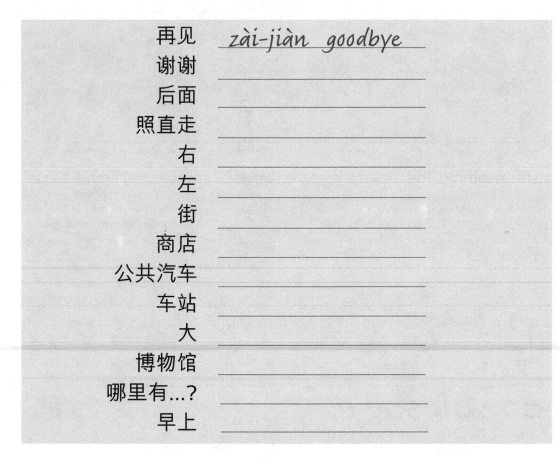

再见	*zài-jiàn goodbye*
谢谢	
后面	
照直走	
右	
左	
街	
商店	
公共汽车	
车站	
大	
博物馆	
哪里有...?	
早上	

Now follow the prompts on your audio CD. Don't worry if you don't manage everything the first time around. Just keep repeating it until you are fluent.

Congratulations on successfully completing this introductory *Read & Speak Chinese* program. You have overcome the obstacle of learning an unfamiliar language and a different script. You should now have the confidence to enjoy using the Chinese you have learned. You have also acquired a sound basis from which to expand your language skills in whichever direction you choose. Good luck!

This **Reference** section gives an overview of the Chinese script and pronunciation. You can use it to refer to as you work your way through the **Read & Speak Chinese** program. Don't expect to take it all in from the beginning. **Read & Speak Chinese** is designed to build your confidence step by step as you progress through the topics. The details will start to fall into place gradually as you become more familiar with the Chinese script and language.

The Chinese script

The Chinese script is not composed of individual letters of an alphabet, but of a series of ideograms, or "characters." This is often perceived as an added difficulty for a learner, but there is also a positive aspect. There is no alphabet to memorize and, by connecting particular characters to their meaning and pronunciation, you can start steadily to build up a basic vocabulary from day one.

Chinese characters evolved out of pictograms used as a primitive writing system. A few characters still resemble the object or concept they refer to, but most have changed beyond recognition. The complete set of characters was simplified by the People's Republic of China (PRC) and both the number and complexity of the characters were reduced. Although the original "traditional" characters are still used in some parts of the Chinese-speaking world, the simplified characters are the most common, and this is the system used in this book. The pronunciation is given in the Mandarin dialect, again the most widespread and the official dialect of the PRC.

Some words, particularly basic vocabulary, consist of a single character. Others are a combination of two or more characters.

A few characters still bear a visual relation to their meaning:

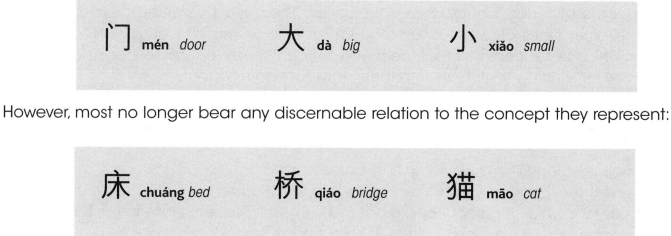

门 **mén** *door*   大 **dà** *big*   小 **xiǎo** *small*

However, most no longer bear any discernable relation to the concept they represent:

床 **chuáng** *bed*   桥 **qiáo** *bridge*   猫 **māo** *cat*

The majority of what we would term "words" are made up of two or more characters in combination. In its simplest form, these combinations can help you to understand the word. If you know any, or all, of the characters making up a word, you may be able to guess at the meaning of the combination.

For example, concepts such as "big" and "small" are used a lot in combination:

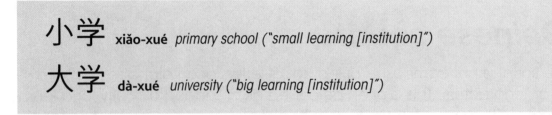

小学 **xiǎo-xué** *primary school ("small learning [institution]")*

大学 **dà-xué** *university ("big learning [institution]")*

and several modern household items begin with the character 电 **(diàn)** meaning "electric":

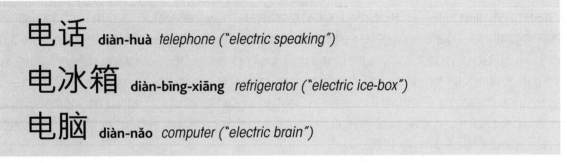

电话 **diàn-huà** *telephone ("electric speaking")*

电冰箱 **diàn-bīng-xiāng** *refrigerator ("electric ice-box")*

电脑 **diàn-nǎo** *computer ("electric brain")*

We have pointed out the most useful of these character combinations in this program as they occur.

The Chinese script does not put spaces between the characters that form separate words or concepts, although it does have punctuation. The period is written as a small circle (。), the other types of punctuation look similar to their English equivalents. *Read and Speak Chinese for Beginners* will help you to identify key characters and to develop strategies for splitting sentences into their individual components.

Pinyin

Pinyin was developed as a way of writing Chinese in Roman script. However, there are some letters used to represent different sounds to their English equivalents. Watch out especially for **z** which is pronounced *ds*, as in *kids*, **q** which is very close to the English *ch* as in *chimney*, **x** which is close to *sh* as in *ship,* and **zh** which is pronounced as a sound roughly between the English *j* as *jovial* and *dr* as in *drove*.

Tones

Chinese is a tonal language. Every syllable in Chinese has its own tone. Mandarin Chinese, 普通话 **pǔ-tōng-huà**, has four distinct tones (five if the neutral tone is included). This means syllables that are pronounced the same but have different tones will mean different things. All the four tones fall within the natural voice range. You don't have to have a particular type of voice to speak Chinese.

The four tone marks are:

- ‾ 1st tone, high and level
- ′ 2nd tone, rising
- ˇ 3rd tone, falling-rising
- ` 4th tone, falling

These tone marks are written in the Pinyin transcription over the main vowel of a syllable, for example 国 **guó** *(country)* or 好 **hǎo** *(good/well)*. Don't worry about always getting the tones exactly right at first since the context will help you to be understood even if your pronunciation is not perfect. After the elementary stage, for which this program is designed, you can be more confident about embarking on the task of achieving perfection in pronouncing the correct tone associated with each of the characters, as well as learning to write the basic Chinese characters for yourself.

You will find some tips for pronouncing the sounds and tones of Mandarin Chinese on track 1 of your audio CD.

1

ANSWERS

Topic 1

Page 6
Check your answers with the Key Words panel on page 5.

Page 8: What are they saying?

Page 8: What do you hear?
You should have checked boxes 2 and 5.

Page 10: What does it mean?
1d, 2f, 3e, 4a, 5b, 6c

Page 10: Which word?

晚上 ___5___ 。

你好，___1___ 好。

我的 ___4___ 黄园园。你叫 ___2___ 名字？

___3___ 陈天宝。

Page 12: In or out?
IN: Jane, Wang Ming, Chen Tian-bao, Claire, Amy

OUT: David, Andrew, Mulan, Huang Yuan-yuan, John

Topic 2

Page 15: Where are the countries?
加拿大 1   日本 6   韩国 7   爱尔兰 3

澳大利亚 8   英国 4   美国 2   中国 5

Page 16: How do you say it?
Check your answers with the Key Words panel on page 14.

Page 16: Where are the cities?

北京在中国。 běi-jīng zài zhōng-guó.

纽约在美国。 niǔ-yuē zài měi-guó.

华盛顿在美国。 huá-shèng-dùn zài měi-guó.

洛杉矶在美国。 luò-shān-jī zài měi-guó.

上海在中国。 shàng-hǎi zài zhōng-guó.

悉尼在澳大利亚。 xī-ní zài aò-dà-lì-yà.

伦敦在英国。 lún-dūn zài yīng-guó.

都柏林在爱尔兰。 dū-bó-lín zài aì-ěr-lán.

Page 17: Audio track 8
John: America; Laura: Ireland; Peter: Canada; Jane: England; Andrew: Australia

Page 18: Where are they from?

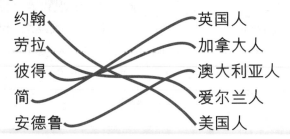

约翰   英国人
劳拉   加拿大人
彼得   澳大利亚人
简   爱尔兰人
安德鲁   美国人

Page 20: Who's from where?

1 他是美国纽约人。
tā shì měi-guó niǔ-yuē rén.

2 她是中国北京人。
tā shì zhōng-guó běi-jīng rén.

3 她是加拿大人。
tā shì jiā-ná-dà rén.

4 他是澳大利亚悉尼人。
tā shì ào-dà-lì-yǎ xī-ní rén.

5 他是爱尔兰都柏林人。
tā shì aì-ěr-lán dū-bó-lín rén.

6 她是日本人。
tā shì rì-běn rén.

7 他是韩国人。
    tā shì hán-guó rén.

8 她是英国伦敦人。
    tā shì yīng-guó lún-dūn rén.

Page 21: Listen and Check

1 False; **2** False; **3** True; **4** True; **5** True; **6** False

Page 21: What does it mean?

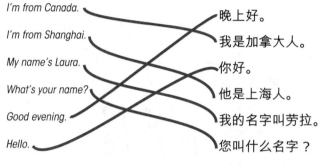

I'm from Canada. — 我是加拿大人。
I'm from Shanghai. — 他是上海人。
My name's Laura. — 我的名字叫劳拉。
What's your name? — 您叫什么名字？
Good evening. — 晚上好。
Hello. — 你好。

Page 22: What does it mean?

1 我的名字叫王明。 My name is Wang Ming.

2 我是加拿大人。 I'm Canadian.

3 王明是中国人。 Wang Ming is Chinese.

4 你叫什么名字？ What's your name?

1 我的名字叫陈天宝。 My name is Chen Tian-bao.

Topic 3

Page 25

Check your answers with the Key Words panel on page 24.

Page 26:
Word Square

telephone, computer, television, sofa, chair, magazine, table, window

直	倕	植	电	话	忍	惹	子
蜘	脂	嘿	耗	鹤	直	合	何
阕	貉	盒	黑	浩	电	妊	蓉
认	电	脑	熔	壬	沙	发	融
纫	视	忍	电	种	岐	炙	子
子	置	椅	中	杂	志	蛊	质
疵	桌	子	丛	匆	电	终	忠
电	雌	凑	词	窗	子	赐	聪

Page 26: Odd One Out

中国 *电话* 美国 * 英国
杂志 * 书 *晚* 电视
木兰 * 王明 * 彼得 *笔*
你好 *名字* 再见 * 早上好
桌子 * 窗子 * 沙发 *名字*

Page 28: What's this?

1e, 2b, 3f, 4c, 5a, 6d, 7h, 8g

Page 30: Who orders what?

Customer 1: tea & prawn crackers; **Customer 2:** coffee & sesame snaps; **Customer 3:** tea & sandwich; **Customer 4:** coffee & cake; **Customer 5:** tea & sesame snaps

Page 31: Unscramble the conversation

h, a, f, d, e, g, c, b

Topic 4

Page 35: What does it mean?

Check your answers with the Key Words panel on page 34.

Page 35: What can you see?

猫 ☑	车 ☐
包 ☐	窗子 ☑
树 ☑	炉子 ☐
床 ☑	橱柜 ☐
电话 ☐	照片 ☑
电冰箱 ☐	电视 ☐
书 ☑	电脑 ☑
车 ☐	笔 ☐
桌子 ☑	杂志 ☐

Page 37: Which word?

1 前面 **2** 下面 **3** 上面 **4** 上
5 旁边 **6** 下面 **7** 后面 **8** 里面

Answers

Page 39: Where are the mice?

There are many possible sentences.

If you can, check yours with a native speaker.

Page 41: True or False?

1 True; **2** False; **3** False; **4** False; **5** False; **6** True; **7** False; **8** True; **9** True **10** True

Topic 5

Page 45: Can you remember?

Check your answers with the Key Words panel on page 44.

Page 46: What does it mean?

小杯咖啡	(a) small coffee
很贵的照片	(an) expensive picture
小狗	(a) small dog
新沙发	(a) new sofa
小房子	(a) small house
旧车	(an) old car
大三明治	(a) big sandwich
大树	big trees

Page 47: Listen and check

1 False; **2** True; **3** True; **4** False; **5** True

Page 47: Unscramble the sentences

1 a, c, b; **2** b, c, a, d; **3** b, d, a, c; **4** c, b, a, d

Page 50: Which word?

1 头 **2** 腿 **3** 肚子 **4** 嘴 **5** 手指 **6** 头发
7 耳朵 **8** 鼻子 **9** 眼睛 **10** 胳膊

Page 51: At the pet show

这猫__2__很长的__6__，长腿和__4__鼻子。

这__5__有__1__头发，很长的__3__和大眼睛。

Page 52: What does it look like?

There are many possible sentences.

If you can, check yours with a native speaker.

Topic 6

Page 55: Questions and answers

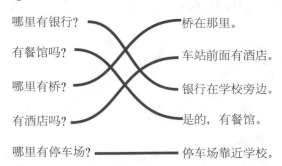

哪里有银行？ —— 桥在那里。

有餐馆吗？ —— 车站前面有酒店。

哪里有桥？ —— 银行在学校旁边。

有酒店吗？ —— 是的，有餐馆。

哪里有停车场？ —— 停车场靠近学校。

Page 57: Word Square

car, boat, taxi, plane, bicycle, bus, train

直	侄	植	电	话	忍	飞	机
车	脂	嘿	耗	鹤	好	合	何
阁	貉	火	车	浩	电	妊	蓉
认	电	脑	熔	壬	沙	出	融
幼	船	忍	赐	种	崎	租	子
子	自	行	车	杂	志	车	质
疵	桌	子	丛	匈	电	终	忠
电	雌	公	共	汽	车	赐	电

Page 60: Which way?

1 去公共汽车站怎么走？ 照直走。
qù gōng-gòng qì-chē zhàn zěn-me zǒu? zhào-zhí zǒu.

2 去停车场怎么走？ 转右。
qù tíng-chē-chǎng zěn-me zǒu? zhuǎn yòu.

3 去银行怎么走？ 转左。
qù yín-háng zěn-me zǒu? zhuǎn zuǒ.

4 去酒店怎么走？ 照直走, 接着转右。
qù jiǔ-diàn zěn-me zǒu? zhào-zhí zǒu, jiē-zhe zhuǎn yòu.

5 去博物馆怎么走？ 坐公共汽车。
qù bó-wù-guǎn zěn-me zǒu? zuò gōng-gòng qì-chē.

6 去机场怎么走？ 坐火车。
qù jī-chǎng zěn-me zǒu? zuò huǒ-chē.

Page 61: Around town

These are model answers. Yours may vary slightly.

the hotel

照直走。接着转右。酒店在银行旁边。

zhào-zhí zǒu. jiē-zhe zhuǎn yòu. jiǔ-diàn zài yín-háng pángbiān.

the park

照直走。接着转左。公园在学校旁边。

zhào-zhí zǒu. jiē-zhe zhuǎn zuǒ. gōng-yuán zài xué-xiào páng-biān.

the bus stop

照直走。接着转左。公共汽车站在
学校前面。

zhào-zhí zǒu. jiē-zhe zhuǎn zuǒ. gōng-gòng qì-chē zhàn zài
xué-xiào qián-miàn.

Page 62: Unscramble the conversation

d, b, a, c, e

Page 63: Game

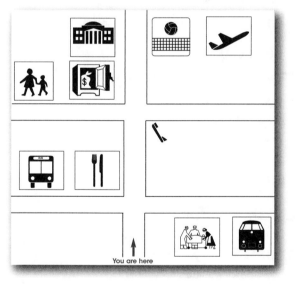

Topic 7

Page 65: What does it mean?

Check your answers with the Key Words panel on page 64.

Page 67: Family Tree

There are many possible sentences.

If you can, check yours with a native speaker.

Page 68: Family Tree

Page 68: Questions and answers

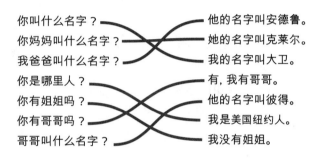

Page 71: How many?

Check your answers with the Key Words panel on page 70.

Page 71: Chinese sums

1 四 2 六 3 六 4 八 5 四
6 十 7 五 8 九 9 九 10 一

Topic 8

Page 75: What does it mean?

Check your answers with the Key Words panel on page 74.

Page 75: The tools of the trade

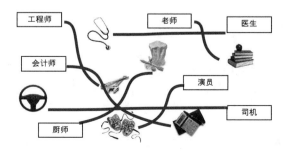

Answers

Page 77: Listen and note

1 *Name:* Wang Ming; *Nationality:* Chinese; *Spouse:* Huang Yuan Yuan; *Children:* 1; *Occupation:* driver

2 *Name:* Mulan; *Nationality:* Chinese; *Spouse:* Chen Tian Bao; *Children:* 2; *Occupation:* accountant

Page 78: What does it mean?

1d, 2c, 3e, 4a, 5b

Page 78: Which word?

我的__3__叫彼得，我是__5__。

我是澳大利亚人。你太太的名字叫

____1__。我们__4__三个

__2__：一个儿子和__6__女儿。

Page 80: Word Square

factory; college; bank; theater; store; school; hospital; office

疤 侄 植 工 厂 忍 惹 子
蜘 脂 学 耗 鹤 好 合 何
阔 貉 院 黑 浩 电 妊 蓉
银 行 院 熔 壬 沙 发 店
纫 视 忍 电 种 崎 炙 子
厂 剧 椅 商 店 志 学 校
医 院 子 丛 匆 电 终 忠
电 雌 厂 词 窗 办 公 室

Page 81: What are they saying?

1d, 2e, 3b, 4c, 5a, 6f

Page 82: Which word?

我的名字叫王明。我是__3__。我是北京人，但是我在纽约的餐馆__5__。

我__1__木兰是__4__。她在__2__工作。

我们有两个__6__，他们是学生。

Test Yourself

Page 84: May I have…?

Use 请给我…，好吗？ qǐng gěi wǒ …, hǎo ma? with the following:

1 咖啡 kā-fēi 2 芝麻糖 zhī-ma-táng 3 笔 bǐ 4 蛋糕 dàn-gāo 5 虾片 xiā-piàn 6 椅子 yǐ-zi 7 三明治 sān-míng-zhì

Page 85: Listen and check

1 True; 2 False; 3 True; 4 False; 5 False; 6 True

Page 85: Which word?

我叫黄圆圆，我是上海人，上海是__8__的一个大城市。我是__2__，我在__6__的中文学校工作。我先生是__1__，他在中文学校旁边的一家__7__医院工作。我们有__5__个孩子，一个__3__和三个__4__。

Page 86: Read and check

1 True; 2 True; 3 False; 4 True; 5 False; 6 True; 7 True; 8 True

Page 87: Read and check

Check your answers with the Key Words panel on page 64.

Page 87: How do you say it?

1 我先生是医生。 wǒ xiān-shēng shì yī-shēng.

2 我有四个孩子。 wǒ yǒu sì gè hái-zi.

3 他的儿子是工程师。 tā de ér-zi shì gōng-chéng-shī.

4 木兰的妈妈是上海人。 mù-lán de mā-ma shì shàng-hǎi rén.

5 我太太的名字叫克莱尔。 wǒ tài-tai de míng-zi jiào kèláiér.

6 她弟弟是演员。 tā dì-di shì yǎn-yuán.

7 我没有姐姐。 wǒ méi yǒu jiě-jie.

8 我有三个女儿。 wǒ yǒu sān-gè nǚér.

Page 88: At the tourist office

再见 zài-jiàn goodbye

谢谢 xiè-xiè thank you

后面 hòu-miàn behind

照直走 zhào zhí zǒu go straight ahead

右 yòu right

左 zuǒ left

街 jiē street

商店 shāng-diàn store

公共汽车 gōng-gòng-qì-chē bus

车站 chē-zhàn station/stop

大 dà big

博物馆 bó-wù-guǎn museum

哪里有…? nǎ-li yǒu… where is there…?

早上 zǎo-shang morning

Name cards:

黄园园	陈天宝	木兰	王明
安德鲁	大卫	约翰	彼得
埃米	克莱尔	简	劳拉

Sentence-build cards:

	我	早上好	你
。	？	晚上好	谢谢
叫	你的	什么	请
我的	名字	再见	你好

Wang Ming	Mulan	Chen Tian-bao	Huang Yuan-yuan
Peter	John	David	Andrew
Laura	Jane	Claire	Amy

you	good morning	I	
thank you	good evening	?	.
please	what	your	called
hello	goodbye	name	my

GAME CARD ③ (see page 33)

Picture cards:

Cut-out pictures (cut round small pictures)

Sentence-build cards:

里	上	下面	上面
电视	旁边	后面	前面
。	橱柜	有	没有
房间	窗子	桌子	椅子
三明治	照片	电话	床
猫	狗	小鼠	电脑

above	under	on	in
in front of	behind	next to	television
there isn't	there is	cupboard	.
chair	table	window	room
bed	telephone	picture	sandwich
computer	mouse	dog	cat

Picture cards:

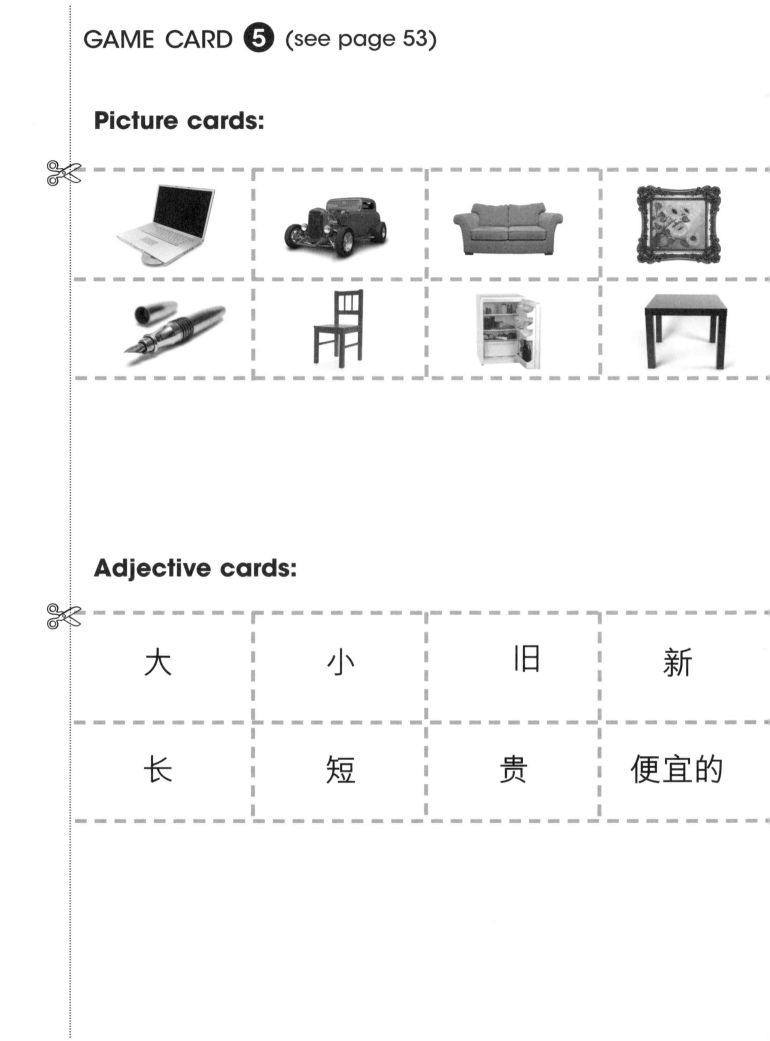

Adjective cards:

大	小	旧	新
长	短	贵	便宜的

Picture cards:

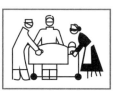

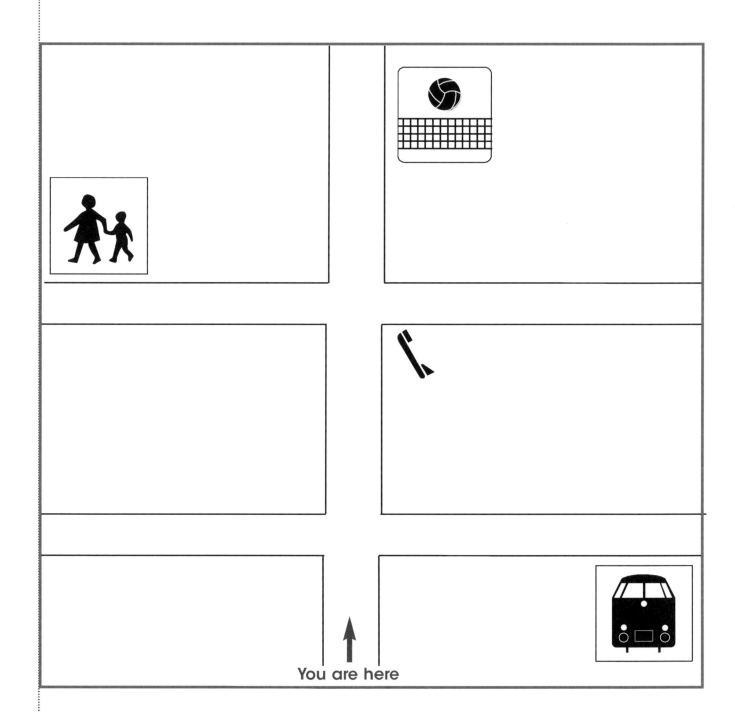

You are here

六	三	九	十
五	四	六	三
一	三	八	二
六	七	一	五

二	八	五	一
三	四	一	二
十	六	十	七
九	一	七	四

一
二
三
四
五
六
七
八
九
十

Picture cards:

Profession cards:

会计师	司机	医生	厨师
商店助手	学生	演员	文职人员
老师	工程师		